Published by
PEACHTREE PUBLISHERS, LTD.
494 Armour Circle, N.E.
Atlanta, Georgia 30324

Manufactured in the United States of America

10 9 8 7 6 5 4

Illustrations by John Kollock

Cover design by Cynthia Davis

Library of Congress Catalog Number 84-60920

ISBN: 0-931948-62-2

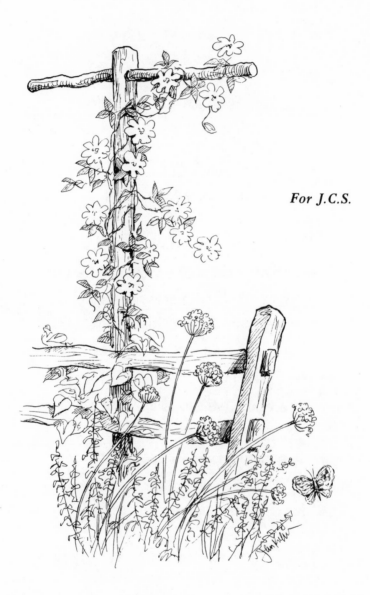

For J.C.S.

Foreword

A MAN I KNOW WHO writes annual reports for corporations is always pleased if he can chronicle a boom year — "productive, cost-effective, up-trend." His language for a season of success interests me. I don't know that I've ever had such a year as some of his corporate customers claim, and yet I don't remember any year I've lived that hasn't been a success.

It's all in the definition, of course. To be able to see, to feel, to be aware, and to savour life is, by my reckoning, success.

Many people have taught me that.

A gentle, good man I met was under life sentence for murder — due to a series of terrible circumstances not entirely of his making. After many years in jail, he was released on parole, and I was with him when he walked out into a light shower of rain. He stood a moment, glorying in its touch on his head and shoulders.

"In *there*," he said, nodding toward the walls he had just left, "you forget what it's like to feel rain."

Since that day, I have walked in the rain, any kind of rain, gladly.

An old neighbor in the hospital, attended by a devoted family and able only to respond meekly when she's spoken to and to offer her wrinkled and wasted little arm for needles and tubes, remembers hard work as success. She held success in her capable, calloused hands when she was out there with her late husband battling hunger and heat and cold, beetles and boll weevils, hail storms and drouths, to wrest a living from a few rocky acres. Her year was "productive, cost-effective, up-trend" when she was able to make a meal for her children from a rabbit or a squirrel and a few potatoes, when she was able to bring down a child's fever in the night, to offer shelter to a burned-out family. She was a functioning, caring, in-charge human being when she called me during an ice storm and offered quilts and hot food off her old wood range to those of us who had no heat and a cold, inoperative kitchen.

The opposite of success is not always economic failure. It is blankness, nothingness, an inability to move, to do, to know.

An old mountain woman I talked to once about herb medicine was in tune with the earth and the weather, sensitive to the seasons. Her grandson, a big hulking man, sprawled on a quilt in a homemade pen they had placed close to the kitchen stove for warmth. He was feeble-minded and very dear to her heart. She summed up the tragedy of his life in three words: "Hit don't realize."

Not to *realize* is the ultimate tragedy for all of us. Georgia's former governor Lester Maddox said of his battle with cancer, "I'm not feeling great. But at least I'm *feeling*."

This book is about feeling.

Mostly.

Oh, it has facts. As an old reporter, I have a healthy respect for facts. Long ago I discovered the writers I most valued were those who could identify a thing precisely for me. John Steinbeck is perhaps the best example. He knew the marine life described in his *Cannery Row* as only a marine biologist could know it. And when the Joads' old car broke down on the road to California in *The Grapes of Wrath*, it wasn't some vague and mysterious mechanical problem Steinbeck reported. It was a burned-out connecting rod bearing.

I like knowing where the months got their names and why. I am captivated by their celebrations. I am curious about the people they gave birth to, the things poets said about them. Some of that is in this book, and I hope also some of the rhythm of the earth and a lot of the feeling for one twelvemonth of time which comes to us all but once and is therefore unique, irreplaceable, sacred.

January

A BEDRAGGLED POINSETTIA, leaning to catch a little thin winter sunshine through the window by my desk, is the only reminder that a week ago this old log house where I live was done up in pine and cedar boughs, garlands, and red bows, ashine with firelight and candlelight, fragrant with the spicy bouquet of Christmas.

In my haste to get Christmas greenery cleared away before the advent of the New Year, I have picked the bones of my little house clean, putting away the tired old 1940s tree-top angel, sweeping out the pine needles, burning — with a great explosive crackle on the hearth — the drying mistletoe, holly, and magnolia leaves.

Why the haste? Why not savour Christmas, as many people do, until January 6, Twelfth Night? Because I'm superstitious, that's why. In the family and the community in which I grew up, we didn't have any truck with the Twelfth Night revels, which, with their bonfires and wassailing, were popular in the time of Henry VIII, and for which, of course, William Shakespeare wrote his *Twelfth Night*. We burned the Christmas greenery so the brand-new year wouldn't catch it in our houses. And then we prepared ourselves for the austere, abstemious, everyday fare of black-eyed peas and hog jowl.

[1]

It somehow seems appropriate to me that New Year's Day should have a lean, stripped down look — no bows and glitter, no angels or red-suited saints, no kissing balls or popcorn chains. The bareness, the spareness of the house seems suitable to a new beginning. Even the plain food, after the extravagances of Christmas, suggests a curb on appetite, a becoming self-abnegation.

Why I should adhere to these notions year after year is beyond me. I know that this is the year's beginning only because a vain monarch named William the Conqueror wanted the year to begin on the day of his coronation. Until then, England's new year had begun on Christmas day, December 25. The ancient Persians and Egyptians began their year with the autumnal equinox, September 22. People of ancient Greece selected the summer solstice, June 21, as the day when their year should commence. For Jews, March 22 was the ecclesiastical year's beginning. And in the Middle Ages, most Christians celebrated March 22 as New Year's.

So we treat New Year's as if it were a day sacrosanct and inviolable, when in truth the things we do today could just as well be done on any other day. We eat those black-eyed peas (with a dime in the pot at our house), assure a year-long supply of greenbacks by cooking and serving collard greens and cabbage, take a painful personal inventory (if we feel up to it), make those resolutions, and divest our houses of remnants of last week's frivolity.

The resolutions, of course, have become a national joke. The tenor is, Why bother to make new ones when last year's are still around, unused and intact? But some of us try. I met a delightful woman who remarked of herself, "I know me and I discourage me." We laughed together, but it's true of most of us. We see our faults and failings not diminishing with the passage of time but merely growing larger and crustier, like barnacles on an old wharf. If, at the beginning of the year, we could take some instrument like an oyster knife and scrape away the errors, the mistakes, the wrongness, starting anew wouldn't seem so difficult.

With that in mind, I asked a wise woman I know what she would do to change and improve herself and her life if she could do it by resolution.

"Forgiveness," she said. "Do you know that the failure to forgive those who have hurt us is poison?"

Forgiving enemies is easier than forgiving friends, she pointed out, and I'm sure that's true, since most of us have more fumbling, well-intentioned friends than we have bitter enemies.

She had one other quality to advocate: honesty. "So much harm in the world is caused by evasions, alibis, and half-truths," she said. "If I could do it, I would school myself never to tell a lie of any size or color. A fib is seldom as harmless as we like to think. It is a chink in the armor of truth. Once you accept yourself as a teller of 'white lies,' you find that the big black ones become easier."

How do you acquire these virtues if they have eluded you up to now? She said she didn't know for sure, but repentance and a firm resolution to change should help.

"Isn't that one of the uses of New Year's?" she asked.

A lot of important Americans began life in January: Martin Luther King, Jr., on January 15, 1929; Benjamin Franklin on January 17, 1706; Robert E. Lee on January 19, 1807; "Stonewall" Jackson on January 21, 1824; and Franklin D. Roosevelt on January 30, 1882.

[3]

Celestine Sibley

It seems to me suitable that our first national election was held in this month of beginnings on January 7, 1789. It was a far different election from the kind that we have today, of course, but it must have been exciting to the new Americans. George Washington, the Virginia planter who had led a ragtag army to victory, asked nothing more than peace and quiet for himself and his soldiers. But he was, in the modern term, drafted. Virginia sent him as a delegate to the Constitutional Convention at Philadelphia, and he was asked to preside. The Constitution was adopted, and he was unanimously elected president by the electoral college. "No other man was considered for the post," a historian reported.

In a note in his diary, the old soldier (he was fifty-seven years old at the time) spoke for the many presidents who were to follow him: "About ten o'clock I bade adieu to Mount Vernon, to private life, and to domestic felicity; and with a mind oppressed with more anxious and painful sensations than I have words to express, set out for New York, with the best disposition to render service to my country, in obedience to its call."

Washington was not inaugurated until April, but nowadays we begin a new presidency in January. It happens only every four years, and it is a memorable time for those of us so fortunate as to live in a free democracy.

"The inauguration of the President of the United States is a solemn ritual in which a simple thirty-five-word oath of office elevates a citizen to awesome power and responsibility," a souvenir inaugural program puts it. "It is an achievement of peaceful transition and continuity through change, the climax of a process whereby a free people select one of themselves to be their Chief Magistrate for the next four years."

The event is tremendously moving, although very simple, unless you become involved in all the parties, balls, concerts, parades, poetry readings, and art shows which have come to be a part of inaugural week. I went to the inauguration of President Jimmy Carter and, looking back, the only event I remember with much clarity and feeling, except the actual inaugural oath itself, was the service held at the Lincoln Memorial at daybreak the bitter cold morning before the inauguration. Martin Luther (Daddy) King, Sr., presided. Leontyne Price, Metropolitan Opera's black soprano from Mississippi, sang. The Atlanta Boy Choir, little fellows with plastic Baggies on their shoes against the snow, lifted their solemn, sweet voices in song. And I sat beside a father and his son, who had come from some midwestern state, arriving at the monument early for a private moment with old Abraham Lincoln. Our feet and hands were freezing but our hearts felt oddly warm, and we smiled at one another tearily.

The inaugural balls have been an on-again, off-again affair. Woodrow Wilson, that ascetic gentleman from Virginia and Georgia, felt that the festive air of a ball "jarred the solemnity of an inauguration." Franklin D. Roosevelt held a ball in conjunction with his inauguration in 1933, but then because of the Depression and World War II, not another was held for sixteen years. Harry S. Truman, the piano playing president who loved a caper, revived them in 1949.

Maybe it's something Calvinistic in me that makes me inclined to the view of that joyless Presbyterian president, Wilson — that the oath of office is the thing, the big and moving moment when the earth must pause on its axis for a fraction of a second to catch its breath because of the importance of the occasion.

The faces of millions of Americans must be turned toward Washington on that January day, waiting and listening and praying that this one will lead us well.

Goodness knows, the oath itself is not a thing of poetic beauty. Its plain words are pretty much the same as those said by country justices of the peace or even the kids who serve as pages in the various state legislatures. But I can't help it . . . I choke up when George Washington's successors put their hands on the Bible and say, "I do solemnly swear that I will faithfully execute the office of the President of the United States, and will to the best of my ability preserve, protect, and defend the Constitution of the United States."

The final words, "So help me God," are not a part of the oath. Jimmy Carter said them, and Harry Truman, sworn in in the Cabinet room a few hours after President Roosevelt's death at Warm Springs in 1945, chose to say them.

It is typical of momentous occasions that some trifling detail will bedevil and distract people. I have always been amused at Margaret Truman's account of the frantic search for a Bible for the urgent swearing in.

"Dad would have preferred to use his family Bible, which was in his office bookcase," she wrote in her book, *Harry S. Truman*. "But there was no time to send someone to get it. Finally, in William Hassett's office, the searchers found a small, inexpensive Bible with red-edged pages, which had been sent to the correspondence secretary as a gift. William D. Simmons, the burly chief White House receptionist, apologized to my father for its rather garish style. But that was the least of Dad's worries at the time."

Chief Justice Harlan F. Stone administered the oath beneath the portrait of Woodrow Wilson. In his left hand, Truman held the Bible and a small piece of paper on which the presidential oath of office was typed. When the official oath was finished, Harry Truman did what George Washington had also done spontaneously.

"So help me God," he added and raised the Bible to his lips.

Margaret Truman has the slip of paper which her father handed her after the ceremony. You wonder if the secretary got her Bible back and values it today, or if it is in a museum somewhere.

Sometimes in January, I am homesick for what was almost my second home for twenty years — the Georgia state capitol. For forty days in January and February, the Georgia General Assembly meets to transact "the people's business." The issues are transitory. What is of pressing, imperative concern this year is often forgotten by next year. But the fact of the General Assembly, its coming together at the bidding of people from all parts of this big state and striving, sometimes valiantly, sometimes half-heartedly, cynically, or sincerely, to act in their interest, seems of tremendous value to me. It is democracy in a form no higher than the ballot box in a country schoolhouse, no lower than the Presidency of the United States. To me, it has a certain majesty.

Of course, I'm a sucker for the rituals and ceremonies. I love the fact that no matter who they are at home, how humble their positions on farm or in small country town, they are "gentlemen" and now "ladies" in this body. "The chair recognizes the *lady* from . . ." "Will the *gentleman* yield?" Since the state was reapportioned, a member is no longer identified by his county's name but by a district number. I still remember the music in the roll call as the clerk intoned the name of the member and the name of his home county.

[7]

Once during the administration of the late George L. Smith of Emanuel county as Speaker of the House, there was a big map of the state on the wall, and when a member stood to speak, a light went on indicating his county. It provided a lovely sense of place. This man was from tobacco country, his opponent from peach country. This was a mountain man from a ruggedly independent county which declined to secede from the Union at the time of the Civil War. The fellow getting to his feet came from the coast. The pert, dark-haired woman was from a little town very close to the great Okefenokee swamp.

That Speaker is gone and so is his map, and so is the roll call of the counties: "Appling, Atkinson, Bacon, Baker" and on down to "Wilkes, Wilkinson, Worth." But the ancient ceremonies inherited from the British Parliament continue. The Speaker departing the rostrum runs to the well of the House, bows to the right and then to the left, and then runs from the chamber (a safety measure in the old days, they say, to avoid being stabbed in the back). The governor may come to the legislative halls and send a messenger to say that he awaits without, but he may not enter either chamber without permission of the body, no more than can the queen enter the British Parliament uninvited. Once I interviewed a visiting member of the British Parliament who was touched and amused that there has been so little change in the procedure which the colonists brought with them from England.

Looking back to the days of my assignment covering the Georgia House, I am certain that I was sometimes bored, often confused, nearly always bone-tired, but there were some excitements and diversions, occasional exasperation at the blindness or pig-headedness of our elected representatives, and now and then the blessed relief of country humor.

It delights me to remember the day I met Cheney Griffin, brother of the late Gov. Marvin Griffin and a member of the House for several years. I hadn't seen him that session, so I asked, "You didn't come back?"

"No," said the ebullient Mr. Griffin. "I didn't come back for reasons of health. The voters got sick of me."

Ah, January. I look at my sagging poinsettia and consider chiding it for not being livelier. It should retain its *joie de vivre* at least through January. After all, it is perhaps a descendant of that famed Mexican weed which a poor child took to a cathedral on Christmas to present to the Blessed Mother. He had no gift but a weed, but so great was his faith, so bright his devotion, that the weed turned into a brilliant, flamboyant poinsettia as he prayed.

Now it lives, for the time being anyhow, in the window by my desk. I want to tell this Christmas flower to buck up, try harder.

We lit no bonfires, engaged in no wassailing as January edged in. We have a measly, Puritan heritage in this house. And the sole record of the Puritans' observance of New Year's was simple and eloquent: "We went to work betimes."

February

OF ALL THE months the U. S. Weather Service could have chosen for its birthday, it seems to me that February is the most suitable. The service came into being on February 9, 1870, and without knowing a thing about the temperature and wind velocity for that day, I am willing to bet that those fledgling meteorologists were buffeted about by uncertainty and a love-hate relationship with the weather. April has the reputation for capriciousness, I know — "The uncertain glory of an April day," Will Shakespeare called it. If he had taken up February now, he would have had a batch of uncertainty to sink his teeth into.

Rain, sleet, snow, ice, thunder, lightning, and suddenly, one sodden day when you least expect it, a sky as blue as Michaelmas daisies, sunshine downright tender in its caress, violets blooming by the back steps, and a faint trace of greenery on the winter-black oaks and elms.

February is crazy, February is nuts, February is a month to upbraid and berate — but only if you're a stickler for consistency. Reared in hurricane country on the coast of the Gulf of Mexico, I have no patience with ever-the-same weather, and I was glad to read somewhere that the great Kansas editor William Allen White had little regard for consistency anywhere. It is, he said, a "paste jewel," cherished only by cheap men. So much for the kind of weather which offers stay-put temperatures and unalloyed sunshine.

My first experience with the weather service astonished and delighted me as much as anything I have encountered in my newspaper life. I was sent as a five-dollar-a-week, summertime replacement reporter to interview the old gentleman who headed the Weather Bureau in Mobile. His office was in the Van Antwerp building, the tallest building in town (fifteen or twenty stories, at least), and I figured that from that eminence he could *see* the approach of all kinds of weather. He almost could. At least, he could forecast the approach of hurricanes and take the steps to the roof of the building and hoist flags to alert the population of the seaport town to get ready.

He might have gone on the radio then. I don't remember. At home we depended on the flags. The youngest children in town could tell the difference between small-craft warning flags and winds-of-gale-force warning flags, and we all boarded up windows and laid in emergency foodstuffs accordingly.

When I met the weatherman in person, it was like meeting Zeus or Apollo, the gods from ancient legend. He turned out to be a grumpy old gentleman who didn't know he dealt in magic. He would have had small time for Ray Bradbury's lightning rod salesman who cried, "What tongues does the wind talk? What nationality is a storm? What country do rains come from? What color is lightning? Where does thunder go when it dies? Boys, you got to be ready in every dialect with every shape and form to hex the St. Elmo's fires, the balls of blue light that prowl the earth like sizzling cats."

No, Mr. Ashenberger wouldn't have cared for that inexact weather talk, and he didn't care for questions from a kid reporter. He referred me to his assistant, a young Kentuckian named Harry Armstrong, who was later to be chief of the weather service in Atlanta and who introduced me to the esoteric-no-longer language of high and low pressure systems and falling barometers. Like so many things television has robbed of its glamour, the Weather Service now has contempt-breeding familiarity, subject to the scorn of every weather observer waiting for every elevator in town.

"What do they know?" we ask one another, shaking the unforecast rain off our shoulders. "They never get it right."

As far as I know, nobody spoke of the fallibility of Mr. Ashenberger, merely smiling a little when he forecast fair weather and appeared on Dauphin Street with his umbrella.

People who don't believe in the Weather Service and have better things to do than bake a cake for its birthday on February 9 have an alternative. There's always the groundhog, due to make his appearance on February 2.

As everybody knows, this weather prophet, whose omnipotence as a forecaster of spring was first brought to our attention by German settlers in Pennsylvania, depends not on sophisticated maps and gadgets but on his shadow. If he sees it, he ducks back into his hole and takes another nap, and there'll be six more weeks of winter. If the day is cloudy and the little weatherman throws no shadow, he will venture out into the world, assured that spring is near.

My friends who exchange weather notes at the elevator disparage most weathermen but *not* the groundhog. I've never heard anybody offer a critical word on him.

Odd, isn't it, that the National Geographic Society says he has been right only twenty-eight per cent of the time in sixty years?

There are other birthdays to celebrate this month: Abraham Lincoln's on February 12 (born 1809); the Boy Scouts, founded on February 8, 1910; Thomas Edison, born on February 11, 1847. But two I favor celebrating are St. Valentine's Day, February 14, and Susan B. Anthony's birth, February 15, 1820.

Even if you haven't a red flower or a heart-shaped box to your name, it would be hard not to celebrate Valentine's Day somehow, someway. It's a day for love. Hug a child, support your local police, give to the heart fund, and be a friend to the library, the zoo, or anything or anybody else to whom you owe a debt of gratitude.

Love, love. And I don't mean just romantic boy-girl love, although that's nice, too. I mean love that sits up with the sick, holds the hand of the dying, is patient with the helpless, the retarded, the handicapped, and even, heaven help us, the boring. I mean the forgiving love of the stubborn, never-say-die Christian who can accept hurts and disappointments and still believe, still care.

There have been times when I have been tempted to pen a vast, all-encompassing valentine to all the people I love. How could I? There are so many of them that it would take volumes. Some, believe it or not, whose names I don't even know, like the black woman I met on the street the other day. I was humming a song I'd just heard on the radio, and she smiled a warm, welcome-to-the-club smile. "You talks to yourself, too," she said cordially.

And there's the man who blows the noon whistle for workers on our transit system called MARTA. I don't know him, but I like him because we're short on whistles nowadays. You seldom hear a mill whistle or a train whistle, a go-to-work or stop-and-eat whistle.

Carolyn Becknell Mann saw a notice in our obituary section, "Miss Morris' Rites Planned: Ex-Principal," and wrote me about another kind of love. The last line in the story said, "There are no immediate survivors."

No survivors? Carolyn was aghast.

"Why, that lady, Miss Avaleen Morris, had thousands of children. I was one of them. There are thousands of us."

She named others who had gone to E. L. Connally school in West End and been in Miss Morris' fifth grade, and she told of her personal experience. She was, Carolyn confessed, known as "a disturbance," the kind of pupil another teacher would have spent a lot of time sending to the office for punishment. Instead, Miss Morris, recognizing the little girl's artistic bent, assigned her to paint a mural in the hall.

"She literally made me an artist. I made the discovery that life would always be different and challenging because of the lovely life of Avaleen Morris and her love and caring that she lived out for her children. She knew every child by name."

There are other teachers to whom most of us are indebted. Valentine's Day is the time to remember them, even if you can't whip up a heart-shaped sonnet or even a scrap of doggerel in celebration.

There will be those who decry the commercialization of the day, as they do many other days. Pay no atten-

[15]

tion. It's love we're talking about, not goods. As some poet put it, in another context, let's be "a little more mindful" of love today.

You wouldn't think it likely that anybody would be blowing up balloons and icing cakes in celebration of Susan B. Anthony's 162nd birthday, but that's exactly what they did in February, 1982. That plain, little, New England school teacher, who was reviled and even arrested for her beliefs, is suddenly everybody's heroine, particularly the politicians'.

It's high time, of course. Susan B. believed so strongly that women should have the right to vote that in 1872 she registered in Rochester, N. Y., and tried to vote to test the validity of the law. She was arrested, tried, and fined, but she refused to pay the fine on the grounds that the law was wrong.

Until women were granted equal rights with men, said Miss Anthony, there was no hope for social betterment in America. She crusaded for the vote and for women's rights to control their own property and to have guardianship of children in case of divorce.

Gradually, some states started amending their property and divorce laws. It was not until fourteen years after her death in 1906, however, that Congress passed the "Anthony Amendment," the nineteenth amendment to the Constitution, providing full suffrage to women.

A salute to Susan B.!

My late neighbor, Tom Fincher, a jolly man who lived up near Chadwick's store, once invited me to visit him and his wife, Ida Belle.

"We'll treat you so many ways one of them's bound to suit you," he said.

So it is with February. It treats you a lovely lot of ways. If you are a sit-by-the-fire type, who loves to be indoors listening to music and reading, February's your month. If you like walking in the rain, sloshing across little creeks, examining the earth in all its moods, February was made for you.

In the little log cabin where I live, twenty miles north of Atlanta, at least three miles from a loaf of store-bought bread when the homemade runs out, with the nearest paved road out of sight (thank goodness), a snowy day in the country is better than a vacation in Spain. Child of south Alabama, I had not seen snow until I moved to Georgia, except for about five minutes in 1935 when approximately forty-three snowflakes swirled through the air over Mobile's Dauphin Street and the edges of Mobile Bay turned white and creamy.

"Ice!" everybody cried, and old Mobilians still talk about it.

Here at Sweet Apple, the little log cabin that was thus designated by old Milton county when it served as the settlement school in 1880, we have been snowbound half a dozen times in twenty years. That's enough to convince me that all the stories and poetry of my youth about snowy isolation were not wasted. There was a wonderful story about a little girl whose parents had to leave the farm for some emergency, and she was left alone to tend the house and the farm animals for what they thought would be one day. They were caught in a snow storm and didn't return for many days, but that child managed magnificently! Food, as it always is with us snowbound ones, was a major concern, so after my heroine had eaten the easy and obvious things in the pantry, she started improvising. I learned to make cambric tea from her — a little sugar, a little milk, a lot of hot water. I gloried when toward the end of the adventure she remembered hickory nuts stored in the attic and made a delicious cake.

For many years I longed to be snowbound, too, so I could emulate that little girl and improvise. I have . . . and I do. The first thing you do when it becomes obvious that there are too many slick and hazardous miles between you and civilization is start cooking. Naturally, you (I) never prepare with succulent steaks and roasts in the freezer. You might have a package of hamburger and maybe a tired, old soup bone or hamhock. Never mind, the trick is to improvise. There's a regular housebound ritual which I glory in.

First, you fill the nearest bird feeder — in my case, a wide board placed over the flowerbox outside the kitchen window, inches from sink and counter. That assures you diversion and elegant, feathered company while you cook. All kinds of birds show up at a feeder on a snowy day, but the really picturebook beauties are, of course, the cardinals, who must know that their black masks and royal, scarlet plumage are spectacular against the whiteness.

Then you build a fire in the big stone fireplace, a fire such as my late friend Richard McKay used to build. Mac was the younger son in a big Alabama farm family, and he was assigned early the firebuilding chore while his older brothers coped with livestock and crops. He made an art of it, constructing in the mornings fires which would last his mother and sisters all day long. He began with a little core of fat pine, followed, later on when he lived in the city, by a lump or two of coal. This made a hot and lasting fire to warm and dry and feed the teepee of green hardwoods he erected above it. One of

Mac's fires would indeed last you all day long, and
that's important on a snowbound day, because you
might not be able to bring any more wood indoors.
Sometimes the snow covers the woodpile. Sometimes it
freezes log to log, and even a strong woman with a
sledge hammer in hand is hard-pressed to separate
them.

Next you check the larder. That hamburger meat can
be stretched into a meat pie. (There's always a limp
carrot or two and a desiccated stalk of celery in everybody's refrigerator.) Add onions, potatoes, a bell pep-
per if you have one, enfold everything in your best pie
crust, and that listless little package of hamburger will
feed a small sized multitude for a couple of meals. Soup
bones, if you were beforehanded and stocked them, are
a great bonanza. I like vegetable soup, and whatever's in
the refrigerator can be pieced out and supplemented —
a package of frozen beans from last summer's garden, a
can of tomatoes, peas, corn, carrots, or whatever. It
smells heavenly as it simmers on the back of the stove
and will be rich and sustaining for many housebound
days. If you're short on vegetables, there are dried
beans or split peas or the pastas — macaroni, noodles,
even spaghetti. In fact, if you have a little cream and
butter and can find your parsley under its covering of
snow in the backyard, you can feast sumptuously on
pasta for the duration.

I love to make bread on a cold day, and there are so
many recipes loose in the world today that you can
have a picnic trying two or three of them. One of my
favorites, dug out of a magazine recently, calls for
cheese, green onions, bread crumbs, an egg, dill, and a
shot of hot sauce to be stirred up and spread over a sheet
of dough after its first rising. Then you roll it up, pinch
the ends together, let it rise again, and cook it in a bundt
pan, which you have greased and sprinkled with sesame

seeds. It comes out looking like a Christmas cake, the seasonings laced through it in a green-gold ribbon, and it tastes marvelous with your soup.

You may not think of making a dessert for your family for months on end, but come that February blizzard, you discover that everybody craves something sweet. What to make? You're running low on butter. Most of the flour has gone into the bread. It's a cinch that at my house we don't have a cache of hickory nuts in the attic, being host to a colony of squirrels. Jell-O is good enough for me, but it reminds my children of school lunch at Clark Howell kindergarten. So we rummage. Down in the bottom of the vegetable drawer in the refrigerator are three lemons.

Enough for a pie? I suddenly remember a letter a Swiss woman wrote *Gourmet* magazine last fall. She begged the recipe for that great American delicacy, lemon meringue pie.

It interested me because I thought Switzerland, like Germany and France, must have the best pastry and pie cooks in the world. Unsurprised, the *Gourmet* writer obliged, and the recipe certainly sounded simple — if I could find it and if I had enough eggs. I found it, and there were the four essential eggs.

With the fire burning on the hearth, the oven warming and perfuming the kitchen, and something good on the record player, you peel and stir and whip happily for most of the morning. Even the birds, gorging themselves at the feeder, make you feel like that virtuous woman in Proverbs who "looketh well to the ways of her household and eateth not the bread of idleness."

But don't get complacent. February, like I said, is tricky. You think you are snug and busy and happy in your little house in its Christmas setting. Then the power, always subject to sudden death from falling limbs and ice-freighted lines, goes off. There you are, your oven cooling, the furnace slipping into a coma, every dish and pot and pan and spoon and plate in the kitchen dirty, and the water's off!

The record player has come to a screeching halt, and even the birds at the feeder have started fighting. There are a couple of things you can do: (1) sit by the fire and knit, or (2) fill your hot-water bottle from the diminished water supply in the kettle and get in bed and read.

You may think you are suffering from the reader's chronic complaint — you've read up your supply of promising books, or you are not in the mood for what you see on hand. Go back to the bookshelves and blow the dust off the poetry.

"White sky over the hemlocks bowed with snow," wrote Edna St. Vincent Millay in the eminently appropriate "Buck in the Snow." "Saw you not at the beginning of evening / The antlered buck and his doe?"

You are off on old favorites. Maybe Millay, maybe Dylan Thomas writing of "the bandaged town . . . the ice cream hills" in a Welsh city snowfall. By the time twilight settles in, making purple shadows on the snow, you'll echo the lines from Rupert Brooke:

> *The kindliness of sheets, that soon*
> *Smooth away trouble; and the rough male kiss*
> *of blankets.*

One good thing to remember is that if you keep your fire in the fireplace alive, you can heat your soup pot on coals raked out to the edge of the hearth. (My mother once cooked a fat hen and a pot of dumplings by this method.)

And the country silence, with none of the household machinery humming or clicking, no television braying, maybe even the telephone silent, is balm to your soul. You listen to a log settle on the hearth, an icy pine bough creak against the roof, and you push your feet against the beneficent warmth of your hot-water bottle and feel gratitude to capricious old February.

March

CHAUCER SAID that March was the month "in which the world bigan, / That highte March, whan god first maked man." I don't know what he meant by "highte," but it's easy for me to believe that our Creator was seized by a great burst of creative energy in this lovely month when the earth trembles on the brink of spring.

According to the calendar, spring's arrival is slated for March 20, but there's no guarantee that calendar spring will produce breaking buds and warm sunshine. I have known it to bring, even to north Georgia, snow and ice. And in Virginia, Thomas Jefferson wrote James Monroe in March 1794:

"Our winter was mild till the middle of January, but since the 22nd of that month, when my observations began, it has been, twenty-three mornings out of forty-nine, below the freezing point, and once as low as fourteen degrees. It has also been very wet. Once a snow of six inches, which lay five days, and lately a snow of four inches, which laid on the plains four days. There have been very few ploughing days since the middle of January, so that the farmers were never back-warder in the preparations."

Many of us are in the same boat — "never back-warder" in our readiness to greet the new season. We

[25]

can sympathize with Mr. Jefferson when he wrote a little later of the "dreadful confusion" in trying to finish his beautiful Monticello. The housekeeping chores we feel impelled to tackle could well be delayed, as the Jeffersons' were by "remarkable winds" in March 1796 and twenty-six-degree temperature.

But who washes windows when, as Jefferson noted, "our peach blossoms are just opening"? It's a time for thinking about the earth, getting off those seed orders (if you didn't do it in February), and hurrying to start plants indoors.

Thalassa Cruso, the garden writer and television personality, is not as sold on March as I am. She called it a month of "considerable frustration — so near spring and yet across a great deal of the country, the weather is still so violent and changeable that outdoor activities in our yards seem light years away." A bit later on she calls it "loathesome March," which irritates me. If it is the month when the world "bigan," the least we can do is to start a few projects of our own, and my favorite is to "bigan" a garden.

Tomato seeds may reliably be planted in flats. Mrs. Cruso suggests egg shells filled with potting soil, then set back in their carton. If you want to involve your children and grandchildren in this project, you can fill an old salt shaker with soil, she said, and let the children cover the seeds. And when the plants reach transplanting size, you stick eggshell and all in the ground.

If you haven't saved your eggshells or don't want to bother with that project, foil pie plates with holes punched through the bottoms, and here and there along the sides for ventilation as well as drainage, are great flats for starting all flower seeds. Mound your potting soil a little higher in the middle, mark off rows for your seeds, sift them in, wet them, cover them with plastic to retain the moisture, set them in a cool room, and stand back.

If you crave a little spring in the house before it has put in an appearance out-of-doors, you can cut wands of any flowering shrub you have and speed up that flowering by bringing them indoors and putting them in water in a dark, cool place. Some experts advocate crushing the bottom stems to facilitate water absorption, but I've almost always skipped that and still had forsythia and flowering quince blooming in the house a week or two before they bloomed outside. They brighten the house and lift the spirits until spring has actually set foot on earth.

March is the birthday month of Alexander Graham Bell (March 3, 1847), Andrew Jackson (March 15, 1764), and of the Girl Scouts (March 12, 1912). But the day which gets the lion's share of celebration is not a birthday at all but the day of a death — St. Patrick's Day, March 17.

For a long time I thought St. Patrick was a legendary figure like St. Nicholas, and there is a lot about him which is happy fancy, unverified but fun to believe, like the story that he charmed the snakes out of Ireland. According to the tale, St. Patrick was such a winsome fellow that the reptiles followed him right down to the seashore, where they presumably suicidally toppled into the ocean and were drowned. A highly impractical theory, of course, but did you ever see a snake in Ireland?

Bishop Fulton Sheen uncovered some facts about the patron saint of Ireland. He was born in 389 at Bannavem, which may have been in England near the Severn estuary, or in Scotland near the modern city of Dumbarton. His British name was Sucat, Latin for Patrick. Strangely enough, he got to the country which reveres him by capture and slavery. Irish pirates, according to Bishop Sheen, seized St. Patrick when he was a lad of sixteen and carried him back to the Emerald Isle, where he tended the flocks of a chieftan of Ulster and was a slave for six years.

"Six years of slavery made him a devoted Christian," Bishop Sheen wrote, without explaining how or why. In any case, the young man escaped to France, where he became a monk. In 432 a vision led him to return to Ireland as a missionary.

"He worked zealously in various parts of the island for the rest of his life," the bishop related. "His labors were so successful that he came to be known as one who 'found Ireland all heathen and left it all Christian.' Saint Patrick founded over three hundred churches and baptized more than 120,000 persons."

For weeks now, faithful fans of the priest have been preparing for the "wearin' of the green" this month and for gigantic St. Patrick's Day parades in many cities. The day became a time of nationwide celebration in 1854, sponsored by Irishmen of both Catholic and Presbyterian persuasions.

The green shamrocks, which will bloom on greeting cards and in the lapels of even the non-Irish among us, are a symbol you may not know about. St. Pat, they say, used the shamrock to illustrate the idea of the trinity.

There's a sign on my wall, painted by the Sandy Springs artist-historian Lois Coogle, which reads, "Wake Up and Live."

"That's the Easter message, isn't it?" a visitor asked one day. Although I never thought of it that way, it certainly could be. I always have to look at the calendar to be sure when Easter is coming, being totally inept at calculating the first Sunday after the first full moon after the vernal equinox. Sometimes this happens in March, sometimes in April; I have to check the almanac to know which.

The message, "Wake Up and Live," is not dependent on full moons or the vernal equinox. But it might very well be a lesson learned from resurrection and the return of life to the earth itself.

Actually, the sign is the title of a book which I like very much. It was written by Dorothea Brande and published in 1935 by Simon and Schuster. I am sure that it has been out of print for many years. I first encountered it in the library, but my friend the murder mystery writer (and indefatigable junker), Genevieve Holden, subsequently found me an old, well-marked copy in a second-hand store. I reread it every few years.

It is invaluable for a writer, because it shakes you out of any inclination to procrastinate, to fool around polishing the candlesticks or repotting the ivy as an escape from your typewriter.

Miss Brande says the will to fail is a very real circumstance in most of our lives. We live as if we had a thousand years ahead of us, sleeping more than we need to, allowing ourselves to putter at time-killing pursuits — "fritterers and players and the drudging workers . . . bent mainly on deceiving themselves, on filling every nook and cranny of their waking hours so that there is no spot where a suspicion of futility can leak through.

"Whatever the ostensible purpose may be," she

wrote, "it is plain that one motive is at work in all these cases: the intention, often unconscious, to fill life so full of secondary activities or substitute activities that there will be no time in which to perform the best work of which one is capable. The intention, in short, is to fail."

Failure has certain rewards, of course, and she delineates these, but she quickly adds that success "is the normal aim of man, his proper objective. Energy is correctly used not by spending it to hold ourselves inactive, not by spurring ourselves to unproductive, sterile activity, but only when it is at the service of the maturest and most comprehensive idea of ourselves that we can arrive at."

Miss Brande gives some interesting disciplines. One of the best of her warnings for a writer is to stop talking, complaining, and asking advice and get at the job. And there are a couple I wish I had emblazoned on a sign beside Lois Coogle's pretty, flower-wreathed "Wake Up and Live." There's ancient wisdom in: "Do the Thing and You Have the Power." And there's a bolster for your self-confidence in: "Act As If It were Impossible To Fail."

The field you choose for this effort is, of course, up to you. For a writer, it is writing. Miss Brande says, "Success for any sane adult is exactly equivalent to doing his best. What that best may be, what its farthest reaches may include, we can discover only by freeing ourselves completely from the will to fail."

Gardeners are unabashed copycats. They have to be. Otherwise, how would they learn anything? There are some innovators, of course. The late Herbert Tabor, the tall mountain man of whom I have written often, was the first person I ever saw to install a gallon can watering system for his tomatoes. He started with scrubbed oil cans begged from the neighborhood filling station, back before plastic milk jugs came along. He adopted the milk jugs as soon as they were in sufficient supply, and in each of these he made a tiny hole near the bottom so that when they were filled with that cool, mountain spring water, they would gently and slowly release it drop by drop into the earth beside each plant.

But even innovator that he was, he borrowed ideas from his mountain neighbors or called upon ancient country lore. For one thing, he was never without martin houses to bring those feathered consumers of insects into his garden. And he early installed a ram in the creek at the bottom of the slope, on which his garden grew, to pump water up to the patch when a season of drouth arrived.

Copycatting is not always easy, of course. I have shamelessly aped my neighbor, Mac, in his practice of putting down sections of the newspaper and mulching over that. *The Atlanta Constitution*, I regret to say, does not turn back the contumacious nut grass. I packed a whole edition around a row of bell peppers only to find, to my consternation, that nut grass pushed its knife-like green blade right through you-know-who's printed face. But it helps. At least, I think so.

My neighbor Nan Warren has an herb garden which tempts me mightily. I have had herbs since I moved to Sweet Apple, and I have dallied with the idea of a formal and traditional herb garden from time to time. But organized anything seems beyond me, so I have simply tucked in garlic by the roses, chives and parsley and basil and oregano anywhere there happened to be space. Then I saw what Nan had done with her herbs.

She has a dainty, handkerchief-sized space, surrounded by a picket fence and charmingly planted with geraniums and daisies around the edges. Next are the old ladders used during the construction of her house, laid flat on the ground to serve as herb beds. Between the rungs are the sweet, fragrant clumps of thyme and rosemary, sage and dill. It looks simple and county and altogether delightful, and I went home and looked again at my patch.

Earlier in the year, I cleaned out a bed where we meant to plant strawberries, and I scattered fennel and anise seed, reserving one end for purple basil, which is so pretty when mixed with pink petunias or roses. It all looks helter-skelter and not at all like the ancient herb gardens of England. Southernwood and tansy are popping up between the rocks on the wall by the back porch, and catnip claims any territory it likes. Since it was at Sweet Apple when I came and was cherished by the settlement for its medicinal properties, I live in dread of destroying it. As a result, it has moved in with the beans and tomatoes and has crowded out the expensive all-white marigolds. (Not that it took much crowding. Out of a package of seeds, I got three plants.) Mint is everywhere, an invasive pest. Garlic and chives run it a close second. What the place needs is a *plan*, I thought resolutely, and I went and sat on the porch and ruminated. Mary Kistinger drew me a plan for an herb garden which was so pretty that I framed it. But as for planting it, naturally I did not. It would be too organized for me to draw off a plot, assemble the plants, and put them in any kind of order. Some day . . .

Meanwhile, if my anise flourishes, what will I do with it? The name, I might as well confess, is the reason I planted it. It sounds like Christmas cookies. In fact, somewhere I have a recipe which calls for a lot of butter and eggs and sugar and one-half teaspoon of anise seed.

Would any sane woman plant anise for a half teaspoon of seed? There is another use. Anise seeds steeped in hot milk make you sleep at night. But since when has any gardener had to worry about sleeping at night?

The joggers are out on the road in great numbers this month. Those who found excuses to sit by the fire in January and February are romping out to feel the breath of spring and mayhap trim down the old body for new clothes. I know because I am one of them. I do not jog every day nor even walk every day, but I feel better if I do and more in touch with what is going on with the changing season. I am cheered by the appearance of daffodils around an old house site down the road, moved that the little ensigns of spring remain long after houses and people who built them and lived in them are gone. I like to check the pisissewa under the pines and see if the fragile, waxen, pink blossoms are out yet and touch the arrow-straight branches of the sourwood to see if I can feel sap returning. Sometimes I find witch-hazel blooming in sheltered spots and the buds red on the maples down by the creek.

Always I find that the litterers are out. I know some people who get their morning exercise not by walking or jogging but by going forth with plastic bags to pick up after those sneaking, despicable, iniquitous characters who spread their garbage up and down the shoulders of roads. By the time you have picked up enough of their leavings, you begin to feel that you would recognize the litterers if you met them in the big road. Some of them consume far, far more beer and whiskey and cheap wine than is good for them. I know the brands. Their empties even now rest in my garbage can.

It's incongruous that they bring paper napkins with them. You'd think they'd be the types to wipe their mouths on their sleeves, their hands on the seat of the pants. But then I remember, the napkins come free with the hamburgers.

What else do I know about them? One of them had a baby. Its disposable diaper was disposed of in the middle of my dirt road a mile away. Having neither gloves nor tongs to facilitate picking up this well-used garment, I left it there. That was almost a year ago, and it is still there, cleansed by rains and freezes, bleached by the summer sun, ground into the gravel by the wheels of passing cars and trucks. It is barely recognizable for what it is now, but I know and marvel that a disposable diaper would be made of such sturdy stuff.

It's easy to read much from the leavings of these people. They wear down the grass in the pasture down the road, probably parking there for drinking or courting. I have found the usual odd shoe that seems to get loose in the world rather often. I have never understood why it is always *one* shoe. If you're taking them off, why not both of them? I have found ladies' (I use the word loosely) lingerie, a man's T-shirt, department store bills, a hot-water bottle, crumpled cigarette packs, tons of cork-tipped cigarette butts, and once a full can of air freshener.

The leavings that have really baffled me are a powdered milk carton and a box which once contained a soaking solution for false teeth. Why, oh, why would anybody take powdered milk and denture cleaner down a lonely country road at night?

All the amateur garbage collectors like me are complaining that papers and cans and bottles are proliferating these days. One woman I see pulling a little red wagon to hold her pickings told me that she used to get maybe half a wagon load a day. Now she sometimes fills her wagon twice. She goes a mile in each direction from her house. I was surprised that she covered so much territory with her cleaning.

"I'm an old woman," she said gently. "There isn't much I can do for my neighbors and the people who drive this way. Ridding the roadside of garbage is my contribution. It might even improve my health, the exercise it affords me, if I didn't get so angry at the heedless people who create ugliness wherever they go."

Ah, March "whan God first maked man."

April

I T'S NOT A MONTH to be solemn and diligent and well-doing, you'd say, this lovely April. It's a month for lying on a hill in the grass and looking at the sky, for smelling flowers and listening to birds. Why, then, does it begin with All Fools' Day, a 24-hour season of silliness and absurd jokes? I suppose it is because children who have been winterbound and engaged in grubby, uninspiring school work need to shuck shoes and sweaters, to caper about and play jokes on one another. Grown-ups, apparently feeling that life plays enough jokes on them, don't pay much attention to the tradition of April fool, but ah, how children love it!

Although its origin is unknown, it apparently is an ancient celebration, because an old English book, published in 1760, mentions it.

For my favorite, Thomas Jefferson, whose birthday falls on the 13th, April was a month of urgent business with the earth. He thought of seeds and plants all year, of course. And much of his correspondence with friends all over the world centered as much about the exchange of seeds as it did about matters of state. I have his *Garden Book*, which covers the years between 1766 and 1817, and I read and reread it with the greatest of pleasure. He was a prodigious gardener — venturesome, eager to try all kinds of things, from olive trees to rice — and I was amused one day to read a letter which he received in 1803 from William Hamilton of Philadelphia, beginning:

"Mr. Hamilton presents his respectful compliments to the President & with great pleasure sends him a few seeds of the Mimosa farenesiana, being all he saved during the last year."

Once on my way somewhere else by way of Virginia, I detoured to visit his beautiful and beloved Monticello. A very old black man worked among the flowers at the edge of the lawn, and we stopped to ask him a question or two about some of the blooming plants.

"Mr. Jefferson always said . . ." he began, and thereafter in his conversation he referred many times to "Mr. Jefferson" as if the sage of Monticello still lived there and might walk out the door at any moment.

You can have a fine, informative time reading of the accomplishments of Mr. Jefferson, one of our more imaginative and innovative presidents. But in April, it is pleasant to read what he wrote of his days at Monticello, after he was ostensibly retired from public life but continued to advise and consult with Madison and Monroe in their terms as president.

"My mornings are devoted to correspondence," he wrote in 1810, sixteen years before his death. "From breakfast to dinner I am in my shops, my garden, or on horseback among my farms; from dinner to dark, I give to society and recreation with my neighbors and friends; and from candlelight to early bedtime I read . . . I talk of plows and harrows, of seeding and harvesting, with my neighbors, and of politics, too, if they choose."

Ollie Reeves, poet laureate of Georgia and for a period the author of a daily column of humorous rhyme for *The Atlanta Constitution*, was a great April man. (Ollie was a great man in other respects, too. Self-made, self-educated, he was a linguist, a musician, and the kindest, most charitable businessman I ever saw, traveling hundreds of miles to help prisoners whose cases appealed to him get paroles and pardons and then staking them to a new life "on the outside.")

But as to April, he once told me that it was not only the loveliest month of the year but the one which had been given the best press by poets. Perhaps because he was the father of daughters, his favorite lines from William Shakespeare were,

> *Thou art thy mother's glass, and she in thee*
> *Calls back the lovely April of her prime.*

What a way to tell a girl, he said, that she's "the spittin' image of her ma" or, as we used to say in the South, that she "favors" her mother.

Ollie knew Shakespeare well. He once told me that during the Depression he hit New Orleans job hunting. There were no jobs, however, and he spent weeks living on a park bench, reading poetry, and subsisting on bananas which were available free at the fruit dock.

"Didn't hurt me," he said cheerfully. "Probably did me good. But it sure as hell impaired my taste for bananas."

Because of his friendship (born of desperation) with Shakespeare, he memorized great swatches of the tragedies and the comedies and nearly all the sonnets. So if the subject was April, he had the bard's words for it on the tip of his tongue:

Celestine Sibley

O! how this spring of love resembleth
The uncertain glory of an April day.

Or:

For you have I been absent in the spring,
When proud-pied April, dress'd in all his trim,
Hath put a spirit of youth in every thing.

And those agricultural lines from "The Tempest" spoken about Ceres, "most bounteous lady," with a rundown on wheat, rye, barley, vetches, turfy mountains, nibbling sheep, and,

Thy banks with pioned and twilled brims,
Which spongy April at they hest betrims.

Showery April can certainly get "spongy," but I've had trouble with those "pioned and twilled brims" for years. I forgot to ask Ollie, who most surely would have known, but I can guess that "twilled" could mean "trenched."

Ollie was right about April's press. Everybody who puts ink to paper about it gets carried away. As much as I enjoy Edna St. Vincent Millay, I indict her for more interest in her words than in accuracy when in "Second April" she called this luminous month an idiot babbling down the hill and a goose girl. More accurate (also hackneyed?) from anonymous sources:

April's coming up the hill
All the spring is in her train,
Led by shining ranks of rain.

Or:

April is here!
Listen, a bluebird is caroling near!
Low and sweet is the song he sings,
As he sits in the sunshine with folded wings.

Or:

Gladness is born of the April weather,
And the heart is as light as a wind-tossed
feather.

Not all of us were nurtured on Shakespeare in the lean days of the Depression. Worse luck, some of us didn't know the rewards of reading poetry at all. I thought my mother wrote poetry when she wrote rhymes, and she wrote a lot of those—limericks for the Sunday newspaper and *Liberty* magazine's contests, and quantities of Burma Shave ads for the roadside signs which were so edifying to motorists in the thirties and forties. We had some *real* poetry in the house, I suppose. I remember a moldy volume from which we read aloud the stirring adventures of Tennyson's Enoch Arden on rainy days and the harrowing "Rime of the Ancient Mariner."

But for most country children in my day, hymns were our first real poetry. I got to thinking about them not long ago when my son, looking up from a crossword puzzle he was working, asked the four-letter name of the mountain from which Moses saw the promised land.

With that letter limitation it couldn't be Pisgah, I realized, and I went about the kitchen stirring pots and racking my brain. "Nemo?" he asked, and suddenly I remembered, Nebo, of course. But since he had mentioned Moses and his exodus, I got to worrying about where it was that the singer in the old hymn stood and "cast a wishful eye." Suddenly it hit me:

> On Jordan's stormy banks
> I stand
> And cast a wishful eye
> At Canaan's fair and happy land
> Where my possessions lie.

It's a grand, picture-making old hymn, and I went around singing it to myself all morning, taking a great deal of pleasure in the words, even if my rendition of the tune left a great deal to be desired.

We were lucky, we country children, to be raised on bouncy old hymns. City churches usually have choirs to sing more dignified songs, and they are beautiful and inspiring. When Fletcher Wolfe sets the Roswell Presbyterian church choir to singing, "Joyful, Joyful We Adore Thee," it's so beautiful I want to cry. But there is active participation in the country churches where everybody bounds in, raising their voices — good, bad, and sometimes terrible — in what we conceive to be a joyful noise unto the Lord. Children learn the words by rote, and grand words they can be. I still remember the surge of pleasure when we bellowed, "I'm dwelling in Beulah Land" and the basses came in with "Praise God!"

At Creola schoolhouse, where church was held on first Sundays, the imagery of the hymns was a lovely contribution to lives that sometimes had little of beauty in them. I remember singing about Cherubim and Seraphim "casting down their golden crowns beside a glassy sea." I didn't know who Cherubim and Seraphim were, of course. They could have been some of that strange, dark-eyed tribe of Slovaks who settled up near Buck's Crossing, for all I knew. But I loved the picture of them "falling down before Thee, Who were and art and evermore shalt be."

Looking back, I probably have been more moved by the memory of my poor neighbors in those precarious years of the great Depression, sitting at school desks too small for most of them and singing — to the accompaniment of the tired, old upright piano — "Be not dismayed whate're betide, God will take care of you . . . When dangers fierce your path assail, God will take care of you."

April has sad connotations for some of us, of course. I thought of that in connection with the old hymns. Anne McFarland, a Marietta friend, wrote me that "On Jordan's Stormy Banks I Stand" will always be a dirge to her, because they sang it at a creek baptizing when her brother came home on leave from fighting with the Marines in Germany in 1917. It was his last visit home before he was killed.

The United States entered that war in the enchanting month of April, it happens, April 6. By coincidence, the beginning of the Spanish American War was also in this month, April 21, 1898.

One of the good April things to remember is that Paul Revere made his famous ride on the night of the 18th, 1775. There were the British at Boston, and there were the American military stores at Concord about twenty miles away. The British General Gage had eight hundred redcoats ready to destroy the stores and arrest the "archrebels" Samuel Adams and John Hancock. Paul's assignment was to ride forth in what may have been gentle April darkness and arouse the countryside.

Revere, as Longfellow's long narrative poem

recounted it,

> *Said to his friend, If the British march*
> *By land or sea from the town tonight,*
> *Hang a lantern aloft in the belfry arch*
> *Of the North church tower as a signal light —*
> *One if by land and two if by sea;*
> *And I on the opposite shore shall be*
> *Ready to ride and spread the alarm*
> *Through every Middlesex village and farm,*
> *For the country folk to be up and to arm.*

Every school child (I hope) knows the outcome.

An April event which I take to heart is the publication of the first United States newspaper on April 24, 1704. They had newspapers in China as early as the sixth century, and Rome had a paper called Daily Events (*Acta Diurna*) in A.D. 476. There was an attempt to start a monthly paper in Boston in colonial days. It had a nice name, *Publick Occurrences, Both Foreign and Domestick*, but it didn't last long because it displeased the local authorities and they succeeded in suppressing it. The *Boston News-Letter*, which was founded in April 1704, also displeased authorities, as any good paper did, but it survived for seventy-two years.

As one who considers newspapers the greatest of civilization's institutions and newspaper work not only a high calling, on a par with medicine and the ministry, but the most interesting occupation in the world, I gladly get up off a grassy hill under an azure sky and go forth to celebrate the April day of its first toehold in America.

An April event which doesn't warrant the national calendars is still reverently, nostalgically observed in the South — Confederate Memorial Day, April 26. A handful of women started it in Georgia with the organization of the Ladies Memorial Association. I choke up when I think about those women, especially those in Atlanta, the most war-torn of American cities. They hitched up horses, mules, whatever they could find, and went out to the battlefield and brought home the bodies of their dead and buried them themselves.

The custom of putting flowers on the graves on April 26 continues today. When I was a child in Mobile, there were still a few Confederate veterans left. They donned their gray uniforms and rode in the parade to Magnolia Cemetery. All of us watching cried unashamedly when one old gentleman lifted a bugle and tried to play "Taps" as the Stars and Bars were lowered at the end of the ceremony. The sad notes were as feeble as he, quavering, dying. Somebody signalled to a Boy Scout, who stood near. He gently relieved the old veteran of his bugle and finished playing the most poignant of military tunes.

Having been reared on the works of Father Abram J. Ryan, "the poet priest of the South," I have never had the stomach for the mock, humorous "Fergit hell!" feud that springs up occasionally, especially in the wares of roadside tourist stands, where you can buy Confederate flags and plates and mugs bearing the likeness of a silly old sport in a Confederate uniform. Recently, knowing my little grandson's admiration for the "Dukes of Hazzard," which I have never seen, I ordered for David's birthday a cake purported to be "real Duke." It came in the shape of an automobile and, I was horrified to see, had a Confederate flag stretched across the top in icing!

It was too late to scrape off the flag and start over, and

David is, in any case, too young to understand. But I got down a moldy old book of Father Ryan's poems, published in Mobile in 1879, and reread "The Conquered Banner," which he must have written a dozen years before at the end of the Civil War. It's a long poem, and the redheaded priest whose brother, Capt. David Ryan, died fighting for the Confederacy plainly loved "the bonny blue flag" and did not want to see it scorned or frivolously treated.

> *Furl that banner! True tis gory,*
> *Yet 'tis wreathed around with glory,*
> *And 'twill live in song and story*
> *Though its folds are in the dust;*
> *For its fame on brightest pages,*
> *Penned by poets and by sages*
> *Shall go sounding down the ages —*
> *Furl its folds though now we must*
> *Furl that Banner, softly slowly,*
> *Treat it gently — it is holy —*
> *For it droops above the dead.*
> *Touch it not — unfold it never,*
> *Let it droop there, furled forever,*
> *For its people's hopes are dead!*

I think Father Ryan would be surprised to find its people have rallied splendidly in the last hundred years and now put the flag in sugary icing on birthday cakes.

In Georgia, April used to be the month when the Irish horse traders came back. An itinerant band of Irishmen roamed the country all year, sending their dead back to Atlanta to the old Bond Funeral Home to be held for burial in April. Weddings were also deferred until the Atlanta gathering at the Catholic Church of the Immaculate Conception.

A few years ago I talked to a priest there, who said the nomads still come back in April but not in the numbers of the old days. Horse trading is off, and whatever business engrosses them now can be handled in a few days' trip by plane or automobile. The mass funerals and weddings are no more.

Thomas H. Frier, publisher of the *Douglas Enterprise* down in Coffee County, Georgia, talked to people who remembered well when ten thousand mostly mule traders roamed the southeastern United States. One old lady remembered seeing thirty of their green tents pitched in a pine thicket every April. Ducks and geese were prepared for their wedding feasts, and there was music and dancing.

The Rev. Frederick V. Gilbert, who was pastor of St. Paul's Catholic Church in Douglas during those years, said, "It was not strange to see sixty or more lined up before a tent waiting to go to confession. The priest sat back of a colored curtain, and the penitent kneeled on the pine needle floor. Surely the devil must have taken flight when those three hundred held lighted candles under the pines and renewed their baptismal promises with the fervor of the saints of the Emerald Isle."

There are many things to celebrate and to accomplish in April, but I could wish for everybody one small benison — a creek bank to explore.

We discovered one we hadn't seen before on an afternoon in mid-April — a little stream and probably an old one, judging from the ravine it has cut through our neighbor's, the late Denver Cox, field and woods and judging from the size of the trees which shade it. I hadn't known it was there until my grandson, Bird, and I went poking around the woods one afternoon. First there's the little gully and then, almost miraculously, the perfectly dry and rocky ditch becomes a bright, gleaming little stream. The journey it makes is a delight — chattering over rocks, swirling around ferny islands, leaping and falling sometimes a distance of ten feet. The banks are deep and cool and green with moss, like secret caves in some places, and then it becomes a shallow, jumpable little stream again. In one wonderful place, there is a tree growing just right to offer a broad and substantial branch for a seat directly over the creek.

And everywhere spring pushes to clothe the tired old earth with life and sweetness.

The dogwood bloom in Atlanta is bound to be glorious. The azaleas are at their blatant, showy best at this season. Spring in the country is quieter, almost muted. Woodland dogwood is thinner, less substantial and a sort of ghostly presence. The wild azalea, which William Bartram called "the most gay and brilliant flowering shrub yet known," is not nearly so spectacular as its city cousin. But when you come upon a full-out, flame-colored wild azalea on a creek bank, you know how Bartram must have felt. It seems ablaze with color and fragrance.

More bluets than I have ever seen anywhere star the mossy banks of our creek with masses of baby blue bloom. In the sunny spots high up the bank, where it is dry, there are thick stands of the rich and splendid little flower which children in south Alabama call "Bonny blue flags" but which botanist Wilbur H. Duncan calls crested dwarf iris. Whatever the name, they are beautiful flowers, silken and fragile in texture, a deep azure blue with golden throats.

Violets are everywhere this year, and the urge to pick them must spring anew in all women in April. I know better, but I tried to bring a little of the creek-bank spring into the house. I happened to be wearing a battered straw sunhat, which, lined with oak leaves, made a fine container, and I had a little knife in my pocket. Naturally, I took up a few foamflowers, a fern or two, and a stand of bluets for a damp dish garden. That worked very well. But on the way home I also dug up a clump of birdfoot violets (properly called pansy violets because of their wide and expressive faces). That was a mistake. They droop fast in the house.

Maybe what we love most about April is its transient loveliness, beyond storing and keeping and prolonging.

Easter

ALTERNATIVES, THE organization which seeks to bring less commercialism and more spirituality into our celebrations of Christmas and Easter, chided us all for squandering billions on Easter clothes and Easter bunnies.

Why not, asked this group, wear common work clothes on Easter Sunday "to better symbolize . . . commitment to Jesus' ministry of healing, teaching, and suffering on behalf of the poor" and give your money to some church to feed the hungry?

Of course, you can't argue with that suggestion. One of the loveliest holidays on the calendar is ours for celebrating, and to give to the hungry is more in the Easter spirit than bedecking ourselves and parading around.

And yet . . . well, what are you going to do about the old ceremonies on which most of us were reared? How are you going to quell the sense of nostalgia that comes when the very word *Easter* means newness and beginning again?

To be a child in the country at Easter-time used to be an exciting thing. The celebration was church-centered, of course. We rehearsed the Easter song for weeks, the non-singers among us coming in strong on the alto in "Up From the Grave He Arose." Saturday

[51]

afternoon before Easter, there was always an egg hunt
on the grounds of the two-room school, which served
as a church on Sunday. Little children got to hunt the
eggs, but, even more fun than that, the big ones got to
dye and hide them.

I remember Saturday mornings in our kitchen when
my mother let me have in two or three friends to dye
eggs. The hot smell of boiling eggs, the brilliant
splashes of dye in all the teacups, and the happy squabbling over original designs were more fun than finding
"the golden egg," which was always a prize-winner.

Then we got to hide our creations. In the little pine
thicket and sparkleberry bushes, in the deep wire grass,
and behind old logs went the dark purple and bright
yellow and sky blue products of our morning's labor. I
didn't learn until I was full grown that the custom of
egg hunts was pagan in origin. We thought of it as
something the church did to bring us all together to
have fun.

Dressing up on Easter Sunday was important then.
Finery wasn't plentiful in those Depression years, but
cloth was cheap and a lot of sewing went on during the
weeks before Easter.

Every little girl had a new dress, every little boy new
white or light-colored pants and a starched shirt — no
jacket. The grownups in our community didn't buy
new clothes much, but they felt obliged to refurbish
what they had. It was a symbol, we all thought, of
vernal rebirth, a renaissance, although we wouldn't
have known the word. The schoolhouse smelled
strongly of shoe polish and hat dye on Sunday morning, richness I haven't seen equalled since.

There were on Easter always flowers on the teacher's
desk, which served as a pulpit for the visiting preacher
— usually wild grancy graybeard or mountain laurel
from the swamps — and it seemed to us that among all

the feast days, this one was a jubilee.

Now ALTERNATIVES wants us to make our celebration "more meaningful," and I am willing to eschew chocolate rabbits and dyed baby chicks for myself and the children in our family.

But I hope most little girls feel the matchless newness of dotted swiss across their shoulders when they sing "He arose a victor from the dark domain." I hope they will have had the excitement of dyeing and hiding bright-hued eggs for some other child to find.

May

J OHN MILTON had some good words to say for this month:

> *Hail, bounteous May, that doth inspire*
> *Mirth and youth, and warm desire:*
> *Woods and groves are of thy dressing,*
> *Hill and dale doth boast thy blessing.*

It is a month that has everything: The weather is so beautiful that gophers come out of their holes to taste it. Old folks and sick folks, who planned to die, change their minds and find "settin' chairs" in the sunshine. Fingerling lizards skitter along the rock wall in my back yard — baby things intoxicated with life before it has half begun.

A lot of us began life on what an old, black friend once told me was the most propitious month of all for being born. "A May child," she said, "get the bes' start."

Among May children are the poet Robert Browning (1812); the president, Harry S. Truman (1884); Gabriel Fahrenheit (1686), the thermometer man; John Brown (1800), the abolitionist; Czar Nicholas II (1868), of Russia; Richard Wagner (1813), the composer; Sir Arthur Conan Doyle (1859); Sir Laurence Olivier

(1907); Queen Victoria (1819); Isadora Duncan (1878); Walt Whitman (1819); Ralph Waldo Emerson (1803); Bob Hope (1903); Patrick Henry (1736); and me (date unavailable).

Everybody knows there's magic in May. Gardeners who can't wait another minute for settled, reliably-warm weather rush to get their crops in the ground — and, it happens, they usually flourish. Sometimes a late frost nips them. Sometimes the still-chilled ground is inhospitable to seeds, and they fail to germinate. But any farmer will tell you, "If you want to plant, go ahead." One of the best farmers I know, a man schooled in the most scientific agricultural methods, once told me that rain or shine, sleet or hail, he planted his watermelons on May 30. There were times when the field was so boggy he had to put on boots to walk across it. But his watermelon seeds got planted on May 30 anyhow.

Children in the South will tell you that May 1 is the day to go swimming, no matter the weather. It is a tradition, an inalienable right, and parents can note an unseasonable drop in the temperature and speak darkly of pneumonia if they want to. The first day of May calls for a token swim, if no more. I didn't know until I visited Germany that May is also a month of religious festivity. A little Catholic church on the banks of the Rhine and every grave in the churchyard were lavishly decorated with flowers — bouquets of lilacs and roses and lilies. And so they would be for the entire month, named for the Virgin Mary, I was told. (Some people, Puritans among them, I imagine, believe that the month was named for Maia, the Roman goddess of spring and growth. Some believe that the celebrations originated with the worship of trees by the ancient Druids. No matter, it's a month to love and enjoy and celebrate in whatever spirit the heart dictates.)

Its association with Mary, the Mother of Jesus, may be the reason a woman named Anna Jarvis picked May as the month for honoring the nation's mothers. She campaigned for it as early as 1907, telling a public meeting in Philadelphia that a day should be set aside to "honor the best mother that ever lived — your mother." Four years later Congress passed a resolution commending the observance of Mother's Day, and a year after that, it passed another resolution authorizing the President of the United States to set aside, by annual proclamation, the second Sunday in May as Mother's Day. In those days, flags were flown from all government buildings, and people wore carnations to church — red ones if your mother lived, white ones if she had died. The carnation was picked as *her* flower because of its purity. Carnations were in short supply in Creola, Alabama, but we joyfully joined the observance by wearing whatever red flower was at hand, roses usually, and tried to avoid the suggestions of our mothers that the best honor we could do them was to bring in stove wood or wash the dinner dishes. Saccahrine poems were the fashion then. Now the greeting card industry, more tongue in cheek than it used to be, kids mama with humorous pictures and jokes about her jolly propensities for fast-living.

Once I wrote a book which the publishers unaccountably decided to call *Mothers Are Always Special.* They're not, of course. I never said they were. They are *sometimes* special . . . special more often than not, maybe. But I never contended that the biological fact of birthing a baby made a slob of a woman into a loving, giving, madonna-like pillar of rectitude. Sometimes the non-mothers who work and sacrifice to rear somebody else's children are the special ones. I have known many of them, just as I have known natural mothers who abused or abandoned their children.

[57]

Celestine Sibley

But as a mother myself, I'm all in favor of a day in which to be extolled (however inaccurately), feted, and gifted. For one thing, it causes you to concentrate for a time on the felicity of having children. I look over my own three and their seven, and I rejoice that I had the triumphs and the troubles of being the mother and the grandmother of the lot. My own mother, who was inclined to cross her eyes and cut a buck step when we came trooping in to pay her tribute on Mother's Day, was certain that she was miscast in the role of mother. As with most of us, I imagine, she felt inadequate to the task, often bored and exasperated with it but unalterably, unflaggingly glad to have us to love and to do for. An only child herself, who bore an only child, she marvelled that there were suddenly so many of us. Once we all went down to her little house in Florida to stage a Mother's Day reunion with a picnic at the nearby lake. I remember that she sat under a moss-draped oak tree and watched the crowd splashing about in the water. To a friend, who had joined us, she echoed the classic line from Louis Armstrong landing among his fans in Russia: "Who these cats?"

There are some pretty awful cliches about *Mother o' Mine*, her virtue, her purity, her unselfishness, and there are some vicious indictments, too. There are smother-mothers, they tell us, who dominate their families, twist and cripple young characters, disrupt marriages, and commit unspeakable crimes in the name of love. In spite of this the children, bless them, are prone to forgive and to do the best they can to understand and to love.

"Why not?" a novelist friend of mine asks. "You *need* your mother, even if she is a poor thing."

So Mother's Day is celebrated, and all over the land we pause and think a little about the relationship — striving, I hope, to be better mothers and better chil-

dren, glad for the closeness, the never-aloneness that
exists for those of us who are lucky in our mothers.

May has not been a halcyon month all of the time for
everybody. Joan of Arc was put to death in May, 1431.
The Lusitania was sunk by a German submarine in
1915. The Johnstown Pennsylvania flood killed 2,200
people in 1889. But there have been wondrous events.
One that is memorable to me happened May 20, 1927.

We were at Sunday school in the little two-room
school house I mentioned, when the man who ran the
post office across the road came galloping into the
building, waving a newspaper. "He made it!" he cried.
"Charles Lindbergh made it!"

"The Lone Eagle," my hero then and for years to
come, had completed the first non-stop flight from
New York to Paris. Space explorations since that time
may dazzle today's children, but for me they cannot
compare with the feat of that lanky, young fellow who
had no great government agency behind him, no millions in equipment and safety devices. He traveled in a
single-engine plane which the people of St. Louis
helped him buy — held together, an old aviator once
told me, by "baling wire and guts" — and was sustained
by a Hershey chocolate bar. He hoped to win the
$25,000 prize which a New York hotel operator had
offered to the first aviator making the New York-to-
Paris nonstop flight.

He won much more, of course — international
celebrity, a remarkable woman for a wife, (Anne Mor-
row, the writer), many awards and honors, and perhaps
the greatest pain a man can suffer. I was a high school

kid hanging around the newspaper office in Mobile when I walked in one day and heard the teletype machine's bells ringing wildly. I had never heard them ring before, and I curiously joined the group of editors and reporters who had gathered 'round the Associated Press printer. Bus Campbell, the city editor peering at the printer, cried out, "THE LINDBERGH BABY HAS BEEN KIDNAPPED!"

It was a tragedy which never seems to end. Even now, long after the death of Charles Lindbergh, the courts have to consider a suit which contends that half a century ago the alleged kidnapper, Bruno Richard Hauptman, was wrongly accused, tried, convicted, and executed.

Years later when I was a reporter for *The Atlanta Constitution*, a photographer (Pete Roton) and I were sent out to the old Atlanta airport on a tip that Charles Lindbergh was coming in there. We saw him land — a three-point landing, they called it in the books I read when I should have been studying arithmetic. We rushed up in time to see him climb out of his plane. To my disappointment, he wasn't wearing the leather jacket and helmet and flapping puttees. He had on a business suit and a hat, like any other middle-aged man of that time. And he wouldn't talk to us. He smiled and nodded when Pete asked permission to take his picture, but he said not a word. He hung around the terminal, a small building in those days, and spoke to and shook hands with airport workers but still no word to us.

We started to leave, but Pete changed our minds. Suppose "The Lone Eagle" crashed on take-off, and we were on our way back to town, somewhere up Stewart Avenue? We went back and waited, and when Lindbergh came out of the terminal, I did something I had never done since I had been a grown-up newspaper reporter interviewing celebrities: I asked for his autograph.

Smiling, he took my copy pencil and my wad of copy paper and wrote *Charles Lindbergh* and handed it back to me. I wonder if it's still tucked away in that little velvet box where I would keep rubies and emeralds, if I had any?

May winds down with Memorial Day on the 30th, now celebrated, of course, on the closest Monday. Except for flying flags and going to a parade, if one happens to be handy, it stands mainly for a nice, long, holiday weekend for young people and those who never lost anyone in our many wars. I was one of those who went to parades, when I was assigned to as a reporter, and gave the day little attention otherwise.

We had relatives or near-relatives in all wars, I suppose — half a dozen great uncles in the Civil War, our favorite cousin's first husband in the Spanish American, a third cousin who was killed in France in World War I. My father, at nineteen or twenty, joined up hoping to "get across," but World War I was a blessedly brief one, as wars go, and he got only as far as a lumber camp in Oregon. So I don't remember being terribly mindful of heroes until I served on a Pulitzer Prize jury at Columbia University and saw a picture of a black veteran watching a Memorial Day parade. He was young, yet he watched from a wheelchair because his legs were missing from just above the knees.

There were a lot of pictures to be judged that day, all of them excellent, but the little group of newspaper people sitting around the table kept going back to that one — the Vietnam or Korean war veteran in his knit cap with a little American flag in his hand. It won first prize for the *Chattanooga Free Press* that year, and I still think of it often, especially on Memorial Day.

Later, four of us were touring Belgium, Holland, and France in a rental car. We spent the night at a country inn and saw from looking at our map that Chateau Thierry was not far away. My father, wistful that his service in the Army had been pretty much what he was doing at home — working in a lumber camp — had talked often of Chateau Thierry and the young Americans who fought and died so heroically there. I am not given to visiting cemeteries in foreign lands, although I love to read the old tombstones in the graveyards at home, but because of my father and my grandsons, then nineteen and seventeen years old, I suddenly wanted to see Chateau Thierry.

We found the American cemetery on a pretty country road near a tiny village called Belleau, where geese paraded down the main street and horses and cows stared at us from green dooryards. It is a beautiful cemetery — avenues of sycamores, then turning to gold, leading to a modest white chapel, and rows of white crosses in the greenest grass I ever saw. But I scoffed when I read the marker about 1,060 Americans, bodies never recovered, who "gave their lives in the service of their country." *Their* country, I thought. France. And who maintains this cemetery? The United States.

That was perfectly true, but later when we met Arthur Martin, the American superintendent, I learned that the people of Belleau gave the United States two hundred acres for that cemetery, the caretakers are all French, and once a year they come out by the thousands to put French and American flags and flowers on every grave and to say their thanks to the men who died there.

"The Names Recorded on These Walls Are Those of

American Soldiers Who Fought in This Region and Who Sleep in Unknown Graves," an inscription on the chapel walls says. I read all the names and grieved a little for the country boys from Georgia, the Alabama and Brooklyn and Ohio ones listed there.

They went into battle with scarcely any training, Superintendent Martin told us. Except for a small cadre of well-trained Marines, they were greenhorns, sent in to stop Germans from capturing Paris. They did it — in two hot days in July, 1917 — and now their bodies lie in the woods on a hill behind the chapel. The French Boy Scouts would like to explore that hill, Mr. Martin said, but it is forbidden because of the very real danger of turning up unexploded shells — a danger which exists in much of France, alas.

We wandered out and looked once more at the rows of glistening white crosses, marking the graves of those who were known, and I thought again of the Rupert Brooke lines:

> *If I should die, think only this of me*
> *That there's some corner of a foreign field*
> *That is forever England.*

This corner of lovely France will be forever America. Mr. Martin saw us out. As we prepared to get into our car, thinking of my grandsons I turned and asked, "Do you have any idea what the average age of those soldiers was?"

He nodded. "Nineteen."

June

"**IF I HAD** to pick a month when nothing much happens," mused a school teacher, "I'd pick June."

"Whatta you mean?" cried her class, rousing from a torpor brought on by the golden, drowsy, pollen-rich air. "School's out in June!"

They were right. Schools close, graduations are held, there are weddings, vacation trips, and summer officially arrives on June 21.

The teacher, as becomes her profession, was referring to important births and historic dates. Admittedly, June has a scant supply of those.

Jefferson Davis' birthday on June 3 hardly stirs up a celebration in the South, much less the North. We give a passing nod to Flag Day on June 14, the day on which in 1777 the Continental Congress adopted Betsy Ross' red, white, and blue creation. Except for any vacation we elect to take as well-earned off time, June is devoid of holidays. And yet plenty happened this month to make us glad or thoughtful or regretful. The Korean War started in June, 1950. The Battle of Bunker Hill was fought on June 17, 1775. The YMCA was organized, Henry David Thoreau was born, the GI Bill of Rights became law in 1944, and Daniel Boone entered Kentucky — all in June. And a lot of musical greats

Celestine Sibley

were born this month: Cole Porter, 1893; Richard Strauss, 1864; Charles Gounod, 1818; Ignor Stravinsky in 1882; and Jacques Offenbach in 1819. Of particular interest to the British is the fact that June 20, 1837, is the day when Victoria became queen. On the same day forty-four years earlier, Eli Whitney successfully demonstrated the cotton gin. And finally, June also is the birth month of King Henry VIII and Helen Keller . . . for those who must have something to celebrate.

But the truth is that June is such a lovely month in itself, it doesn't need to produce an excuse for celebration. James Russell Lowell, who wrote that line, "What is so rare as a day in June?", which high school English students have been memorizing for a hundred years, also wrote,

No price is set on the lavish summer;
June may be had by the poorest comer.

I thought of that one morning when I paused in front of a rickety, decaying, vacant house in a dejected part of town, looking for the address of a retired, black, school teacher who had written me an urgent request to come and see her. I fumbled for the envelope bearing the street number and was squinting at the long-ago defaced numerals over the door of the old house when a man walked around the side.

He was, like the house, pretty dilapidated, but he was not at all dejected. I recognized in his shambling gait and his seediness a veteran wino, a brotherhood with which I have a long-standing acquaintance. He confirmed that impression almost immediately, but first he saw me looking at the tangle of half-wild flowers blooming by the walk — a species of black-eyed Susan that is utterly indestructible and a weedy but very pretty pink flower, probably planted thirty

[66]

years earlier by people who lived in and loved the house.

His rheumy old eyes rested on them admiringly. "Ain't it a fairyland?" he asked, stretching in the sunshine and leaning over to touch a flower.

June. She may be had by the poorest comer.

In fact, the poorer the comer, the more precious the golden climate of June, I imagine. This gentleman camped out in the kitchen of the vacant house, coming and going through a loose plank over a boarded-up window. It had sheltered him in bitter weather, and now he was free to take to the great out-of-doors, to join other street people in doorways or under the viaduct or in the weed patches by a stretch of railroad tracks not easily accessible to the police. He told me a little of his lifestyle, and under the spell of the blue and gold day, his life didn't sound so mean and poor. A poet named Robert Bridges who wrote "When June is Come" might have been writing of him:

> *When June is come, then all the day*
> *I'll sit with my love in the scented hay;*
> *And watch the sunshot palaces high,*
> *That the white clouds build in the breezy sky.*

He and his friends, if not his love, have the scented hay of the weed patches. Those of us who try to garden small, backyard plots have our own weed patches, not to lounge around in with a bottle of muscatel or, if things are not quite that good, a flagon of Miss Peach shaving lotion, but to hack at with hoe and swinging blade. June is planting time and weeding time — and in some of our gardens, weeds always predominate.

Occasionally a gardener is given a bonny June morning to do with exactly as he pleases. I remember standing ankle-deep in the dew-wet grass on such a morning and realizing that I had four, delicious, uninterrupted hours before me — to weed, to water, to fertilize beds already grown heat-weary and weedy. I never had a better time. I assembled trowel and scratcher and mixed a lovely stew of nutrients for the flower beds. That's anything plant-nourishing you happen to have, stirred together in a rusty, leaky, old washtub. My ingredients ran to dirt from the compost pile, peat moss, cow manure, and a sprinkling of 8-8-8 store-bought fertilizer and lime.

There have been people who say the border along the rock wall by my back door could do with a spot of planning. They are crazy. The border is a hodgepodge accumulation, a collection of afterthoughts — and I love it. Those people who point to the precise order and beauty of the wonderful borders and beds we are getting around public buildings, apartment complexes, and stores are passers-by, not sitters-and-lookers. A collection of mellifluously blooming geraniums, marigolds, and petunias, planted exactly six inches apart, is beautiful, it's true. But after you've looked at it, you've seen it. Not so with my rock-wall border. It is loaded with surprises, well-stocked with the unexpected. I never weary of looking at it.

On this great, free morning, I knelt beside it and exulted in its texture, its symmetry. Peaks of bright, gold celosia emerging from a nice tangle of nearly wild dusty miller. (Not the new annual dusty miller, which you buy nowadays — they're one-season plants — but the old-fashioned, perennial stuff you sometimes find around old house sites. It multiplies and returns — marvelous attributes in a flower.) Lavendar, sage, parsley, all cheerfully fellowshipping together. House leek (which was at Sweet Apple before I was), catnip, lamb's ears (which every gardener needs to set off everything else), geraniums, daisies, a few pinks, a trailing sprig or two of verbena, and a cascade of the old-fashioned yellow moss, which came from the old Chadwick house up the road.

All these and more were bound together by a stubborn snarl of grass, but somehow in the early-morning light that grass didn't offend me. It looked lacy, its leaves pale emerald, a sort of horticultural frill for my plants. Nevertheless, I pulled it. It came out willingly. And in its place I served up goodies from the leaky washtub. The garden hose went with me, adjusted to drip slowly and silently on the roots of the plants, and the children's red wagon was at my elbow, slowly filling up with weeds.

The sun grew hot and poured its bright, gold light over the earth like melted butter. The birds, which had been singing earlier, retired for their midday siesta. I hauled leaves and pine straw from the woods down the hill and lovingly mulched the now-wet and weed-free border. In the house, the old clock struck noon. I had just time enough to shuck off mud-coated jeans, shower, and get to my first appointment of the day. No, second appointment. The first was with the earth and June.

June wouldn't be June without commencement. And yet high school graduations, as most of us know them, soon may be a thing of the past. There are more and more youngsters who eschew the cap and gown and ask that their diplomas be mailed to them, taking off for summer jobs somewhere. A young woman at a church supper told me that there was hardly anybody left but faculty when she got her diploma, and even the faculty was restive and eager to be done with it.

"Why?" I asked. "Why would anybody who had worked hard for four years to get that diploma want to pass up the festivities?"

She shrugged. "So what's to like about it? A lot of dull speakers telling you that 'the future is yours' and stuff like that."

I returned to my aspic, chastened. As one who has spouted all the cliches known to man to graduating classes, I couldn't bear to hear any more about dull speeches and platitudes. I wanted to tell her that it didn't hurt us parents and grandparents, who went through it, to hear our elders make hail-and-farewell, onward-and-upward noises. In fact, like the old grandfather in *You Can't Take it With You*, I love commencements.

Do you remember the old gentleman, played the last time I looked by Lionel Barrymore, who went out every June to see groups of young strangers graduate from high school? He felt rejuvenated and restored, filled with hope and high expectations, by their youth and their promise.

Commencements make me feel optimistic and nostalgic. I want to hear the band play "Pomp and Circumstance" or "Coronation March." I want to smell the flowers and see some grey-templed dignitary with a tassle bobbing over his forehead hand out those diplomas tied with the school colors. I like to hear how it's a durable, old world we're turning over to them, and theirs is the challenge, theirs the opportunity, to make it better than we have. Doesn't that impress the young any more? It did me. I believed it.

Maybe today's children are more realistic than we were. I heard the other day about a young girl I know who was passing up commencement festivities and rushing to join the Army. She was done with school —

"I'm not college material," she said — and sensibly grabbed the best opportunity offered.

"Knows her own limitations," a relative said, and for a moment I thought it was smart of her.

On the other hand, there's some advantage in not knowing one's limitations. The large venturesomeness of youth comes to you but once — a brief time when you feel invincible, when there isn't anything you can't do if you but try.

Most of us would have had very tedious and stagnant lives if we have lived and been governed by our limitations. The impossible dream is not to be lightly dismissed. The little I-think-I-can engine of the first-grade textbook was pretty inspiring.

Do they tell graduates that oldie about playing the piano of life with all ten fingers, instead of picking out "Chopsticks" with two fingers? I hope they hurry before commencements are cancelled for lack of interest.

Summertime is family reunion time in the South and perhaps in all other sections of the country, too. It's easier for people to make trips, and the fine weather encourages outdoor gatherings where there is room for all at picnic tables set under trees. Children can run freely, and little babies can be settled on quilts on the grass for naps.

My neighbor was hosting the big clan she calls family on a mid-June Sunday, and I volunteered to bring flowers for the tables. The larkspur and poppies and little perennial sunflowers in my yard would have made meager bouquets for such a big gathering, so I took my

[71]

plastic bucket of water and my clippers and went scavenging for roadside wildlings. It's lovely to be out picking flowers in the early morning quiet.

The dew is fresh and cool, the sun is only beginning to send fingers of light through the pines, and the neighbors are still sleeping.

This is the season of the year for Queen Anne's lace, surely one of the most prolific and least appreciated wildlings we have. It fills fence rows and overflows into fields and lifts its little caps of delicate gauze in pastures and creek bottoms. You can pick blossoms that are six inches across, but, even better, you can find fragile ones that look like a spider constructed them in sizes of one inch.

Up to my knees in Queen Anne's lace, I clipped a plastic bucket full, keeping one eye out for snakes. The other eye was on the amber tide of daylillies which swept up the hill from the creek bottom. It's tricky picking daylillies before the sun is well up, because they don't open until it strikes and warms their secret faces. I thought I could tell a today's lily from a yesterday's and a tomorrow's, but I wasn't sure. So I picked more Queen Anne's lace, a few daisies, a frond or two of fern, and waited.

In a little while the lilies began stirring, a pointed, apricot-colored petal moved ever so slightly, nudging the one next to it to unfold. Within moments I had my bucket full of today's day lilies, open, golden-hearted, and fragrant. The bouquets I made for my neighbor's picnic tables wouldn't win me any awards for flower arranging, but they pleased me. One was in an old, homemade, split oak basket, stained by berries and grapes and time. The other was in a little market basket. The roadside flowers looked so charming that I got carried away and took the clippers to add to their company some of my larkspur and poppies and little perennial sunflowers.

Sometimes in June, I remember the grace-at-table to-do I became embroiled in a few Junes ago. A woman wrote to ask me about the custom of asking a blessing at mealtime. Do people still do it? Is it considered good form when you have guests? If they decided to start the custom for her grandchild's benefit, would I give her a blessing to ask?

I must have fumbled badly without offering the woman advice or blessing in which to sink her teeth, because the mail on the subject suddenly innundated me.

"Shame on you, not having a blessing handy to give that grandmother who appealed to you for help!" wrote an Atlanta woman. "You may have missed a chance to help a family to stronger faith!"

She forthwith gave me her family's favorite blessing, and so did a couple of hundred other people. Marel Brown, the poet, sent me her favorite by her husband's fellow Scot, Robert Burns:

> *Some hae meat and canna eat*
> *And some wad eat that want it.*
> *But we hae meat and we can eat.*
> *And sae the Lord be thanket.*

Mrs. Brown wrote a book for children in which a little boy in the story needed a blessing to ask at breakfast. She wrote for him this charming one:

> *We thank you God, for food today,*
> *We thank you for our Mother.*

Celestine Sibley

And help us as we work and play
Be kind to one another.

The wife of a man from New Orleans said their
family always ended their blessing with "God bless the
cook and the man who chopped the wood."

The Hotchkiss School dining hall blessing was the
favorite of many people:

Back of the loaf is the snowy flour,
And back of the flour, the mill.
Back of the mill is the wheat and the shower,
And the sun, and the Father's will . . .

One of my favorites was written centuries ago by
Robert Herrick and, I'm sure, wasn't intended to be
funny, but I would never attempt it at mealtime because
I think it is marvelously comic:

Here a little child I stand
Heaving up my either hand;
Cold as paddocks though they be
Here I lift them up to Thee,
For a benison to fall
On our meat and on us all.

My mental picture was of a little boy lifting cold fish
— haddocks — but I looked up paddock, and when it
doesn't apply to a place for horses, it is a term for frogs.

Christina Rossetti wrote a nice one with a memorable beginning: "I shout before Him in my plenitude."
To shout in one's plenitude sounds wonderfully exu-
berant. It also has a nice ending: "Of light and warmth,
of hope and wealth and goods; Ascribing all good to the
only Good."

There were many beautiful blessings taken from the

Bible, some from Martin Luther and John Wesley, and one from William Shakespeare, which may be the best of all:

> *Oh, Lord that lends me life,*
> *Lend me a heart replete with thankfulness.*

I bet he wrote it in June.

July

IN THIS MONTH of brassy, hot sun, when the earth turns slowly toward fruition, it seems phenomenal that so many nations, our own among them, mopped their brows and declared their independence. Somewhere I read that a nation's holidays are the best index to its history, its character, and its aspirations. Nine nations celebrate some day in July as their birthday, although the United States is the only one among them that knows the exact date of its birthing — July 4, 1776, when the Continental Congress adopted the Declaration of Independence. Anyhow, the French celebrate July 14 as Bastille Day; the Canadians, July 1 as Dominion Day; the Philippines, our own July 4; Venezuela, July 5; Argentina, July 9; Belgium, July 21; The Netherlands, July 25; and Peru, July 28.

Perhaps the most magnificent and meaningful birthday present anybody, nation or individual, ever received was given to the United States by France on July 4, 1884. The mammoth Statue of Liberty wasn't gift-wrapped. It came in 214 packing cases and took more than a year to be assembled and placed on that little island overlooking the ship channel of New York harbor. I would like to have been there when President Grover Cleveland dedicated the monument and it was unveiled before an audience which included many happy representatives of France. But the first time I saw "Liberty Enlightening the World," the correct name of the woman holding the torch, was pretty good in itself. I had gone to New York to chaperone a couple of teen-age youngsters who had won the trip for their accomplishments in Junior Achievement.

By the time we got around to taking the ferry to the Statue of Liberty, some of the luster had worn off sightseeing for me. I was tired, the kids were tired. We had been to Rockefeller Center, topped the Empire State building, toured the Metropolitan Museum, eaten in Chinatown, tried the rides at Coney Island, applauded the Rockettes, spent two nights in a suite at the Waldorf, seen a Broadway musical, toured skid row in a chauffeur-driven limousine, and participated in a television show. We boarded the ferry with a jaded, "show me" attitude.

The youngsters found seats and slumped down, no longer excited about the skyline. I fell into conversation with an elderly couple standing by the rail on the deck. They were excited by the skyline, and they turned their old faces toward the Statue of Liberty with expressions of reverence and awe.

They were Kansas farmers who had saved all their lives for a trip to New York City to see the Statue of Liberty, of which they had heard much from their immigrant parents. Farming had been a tough enterprise for them, and they had a big family of children, but they put aside a few pennies for the trip whenever they could. The children grew up and left home, and they sold a cow or two and some wheat, and finally they felt ready for the big trip. They made it by Greyhound bus, riding all day and getting off at night and seeking lodging with farm families near small towns.

"We never failed to find wonderful, hospitable people," the woman told me.

Suppose there had not been a family to take them in? Or even a small-town hotel room?

"We didn't worry," the woman said gently. "We could have sat up all night somewhere and waited for the next bus. We have sat up with sick children and sick cows and sheep many times."

They arrived in New York that morning, found lodging, took baths, and headed immediately for the Statue of Liberty. As the ferry eased into the dock, the old woman stopped talking and reached for her husband's hand. Their wrinkled, sun-and-wind-roughened old faces were lifted to the statue in wonderment. A tear slipped down the old woman's cheek, and I heard her say softly, "A mighty woman with a torch . . . Mother of Exiles."

I looked at the old man questioningly. "She knows it all by heart, that poem by Emma Lazarus," he said.

I didn't know it, and neither did the two teen-agers who made quick work of seeing the now century-old statue. The old couple did not return with us on the ferry. They planned to see every inch of Miss Liberty before they left her.

Sometimes on the Fourth of July, I reread the Emma Lazarus poem which is inscribed on a tablet in the pedestal holding the statue. Some of our ancestors got to this country before that birthday gift from France arrived. Others trying desperately to get here will never make it. But for that Kansas farm couple and thousands like them, the "Mother of Exiles" truly said,

> *Give me your tired, your poor,*
> *Your huddled masses yearning to breathe free,*
> *The wretched refuse of your teeming shore,*
> *Send these, the homeless, tempest-tost to me,*
> *I lift my lamp beside the golden door.*

It makes you want to say, "Happy birthday, America!"

A lot of famous people share this birthday month — Count von Zeppellin (1838), the German inventor; John D. Rockefeller (1839), the American capitalist; Samuel Colt (1814), the pistol man; Rembrandt, (1606), the Dutch painter; Ernest Hemingway (1898), the novelist; John Jacob Astor (1763); Benito Mussolini (1883); and Henry Ford (1863).

Astrologists probably could tell us what these men had in common. But beyond reading my Stargazer in the morning paper, I have given up on astrology. I'll tell you why. Once I got very excited when a woman who is knowledgeable about it took what I now realize was a cursory look at my stars and said that I was "alert, clever, versatile, and resourceful." Practically oracular, I decided, believing every word of it. When she added "sophisticated, adventurous, sensitive, affectionate, and refined," I was completely sold.

Then I checked into some of the other signs in the zodiac. Lo and behold, Pisces children are "receptive, sensitive, and compassionate," Aquarians "sensitive, generous, and understanding;" Saggitarians "jovial, pleasing, benevolent, kind, and honorable." And so it goes, everybody born under any sign whatever is splendidly endowed and amazingly alike. But my nose is still out of joint. I wanted to be the only alert, clever, versatile, and resourceful girl in the crowd.

For many years people in Sweet Apple settlement have celebrated the July birthday of Odessa Crow (called Dessie), the widow of one of our best-loved citizens, Lum Crow. He was a tall, lanky, banjo-picking, mountain man who farmed and made a little moonshine, and hunted rabbits and squirrels, and "holped" the neighbors when there was sickness or other need in the settlement. Mr. Crow was one of our first visitors when we moved to Sweet Apple cabin. He had received his only schooling in it back in the 1890s, when such book-learning as the locals got was dispensed here by a $25-a-month schoolmaster hired by old Milton county. The cabin is not particularly light now, and it certainly was dark then with no glass windows. Mr. Crow recalled that the "scholars," sitting on puncheon benches, had to remove the boards covering the cracks between the logs to get light enough to see by.

After Mr. Crow died, we wondered if Miss Dessie would have the heart for the annual celebration of her birthday under the trees in their backyard. When she was ninety-one, we felt that she might not feel up to a party.

"Why, she's not going to stop doing anything she has always enjoyed doing if she can help it," said Jettie Bell Johnson, a long-time friend and neighbor. "Mrs. Crow wouldn't miss a party for anything."

Although it rained, it was a terrific party in the old-fashioned tradition. The men gathered on the front porch, filling the chairs, leaning against the posts, squatting around. The women, bearing baskets and boxes and plastic-covered containers, headed for the kitchen. There Mrs. Crow's daughter and granddaughter directed the placing of the vittles — vegetables and meats here, biscuits and cornbread there, drinks on that table, salads on that counter, and finally, the

crowning achievement of the settlement's best cooks —
cakes and pies over yonder.

Mrs. Crow, dressed in pink, moved among the
guests asking about absent members of families, com-
paring notes on gardens, expressing gratitude for the
rain, even if it had forced her party indoors.

"It's always been so nice out there under the trees,"
she said, nodding toward the grove just beyond the
yard. "But we can do all right inside since we have to."

A lot of us were thinking back to other years when
Lum Crow himself was present at the party, cradling
his banjo in the crook of his arm, tilting his chair on its
back legs, the better to strum out a tune like "Soldier's
Joy" or "Finger Ring."

We remembered the picking and singing and buck
dancing that went on under the trees. But the spirit of
the gathering had not diminished. The sharing of food,
the neighboring, and the good feeling that once more
we could celebrate a year of living for our neighbor
were the same.

Before he asked the blessing, the minister spoke of
Mrs. Crow's well-lived life. But when it came her time
to say a few words, she spoke softly of her gratitude —
to "my companion" (as she called Mr. Crow), her
children, her neighbors, and friends. And then the
poignant blessing which many old people must envy
her — the privilege of living in her own home.

She smiled and paused, listening to the whisper of the
rain dropping off the roof and hitting her boxwood and
althea bushes outside. "I thank God," she said, "that I
can be here in my home, and that you are all here with
me. I hope it won't be our last time here together."

It was Mrs. Crow's last birthday party at home. The
time came when she had to move to Roswell with her
daughter and son-in-law, Christine and Frank Col-
eman, and felt lucky that they were loving and welcom-

ing. We all went to the auction of her household effects. Some of us cried, but Mrs. Crow didn't. When I bought her old sifter for a couple of dollars, she smiled at me mischievously and said, "Lummie give twenty cents for that forty years ago!"

Among the Fourth of July greetings which come my way was one on blue-lined, tablet paper which said briefly and succintly, "The United States of America is going to hell in a handbasket."

The writer, an ex-Marine, did not give his reasons for pessimism, and I didn't really want them. I was in a hurry to get off to the Fourth of July picnic, which has become a sort of tradition among our neighbors. Larry and Barbara Thorpe, a city couple who moved to the country and built a pretty house on a lake a dozen years ago, may have started it. Some years we "spread dinner together" in their yard. Other years it is held in the backyard of Paul and Jettie Bell Johnson, whose families cleared land and built houses here nearly a century ago. We go with our covered dishes and our yard chairs and set up in the shade, where the breeze off the cornfield and the watermelon patch stirs around in the old trees, and the July flies saw out their ancient symphony of summertime and a mellow fruitfulness.

The youngsters may get up a baseball game or swim in the pond. There'll be good talk of weather and gardens and illnesses and new settlers in the community, and we'll linger until after the sun goes down and it's time to go home and take down our American flags for another year.

And it won't seem to many of us that the country's in

a worse way this year than it has been so many times in years past.

Such gatherings as ours have been common in this country for centuries, I suppose. Churches have home-comings and decoration days, when dinner is "spread together" and graves are visited in old churchyards and decorated with wilting flower from home yards.

Political gatherings were the same kind of happy, outdoor fetes until a few years ago, when television made it possible for a candidate to reach more people faster without traveling to the little towns and country places to make his pitch to the voters. I remember going to one for the late Georgia Senator Richard Russell where the smoke of barbecuing shoats and beeves rose in the hot summer air, where old hound dogs slept under old cars, and people gathered 'round to hear the man speak and to shake his hand. It struck me then that it was a wonderful piece of Americana, and I hoped it would flourish forever, the political barbecue.

Tom Watson, the United States senator and populist candidate for vice president, was also a writer of note. In an old novel, *Bethany*, he caught the flavor of such a gathering before the Civil War when two Georgia orators of fame, Robert Toombs of Washington-Wilkes and Alexander Stephens of Crawfordville, debated the hot issue of secession.

"Wagons, ox-carts, buggies, carriages were scattered about over acres of ground," he wrote. "Saddle horses were hitched to swinging limbs, men on foot were coming on every path. Ladies filled the seats in front of the stand, children ran in and out among the benches, babies cried, and many a mother could be seen suckling these infants as modestly as the thing could be done under the circumstances. To the rear of the benches and far out upon both sides, the men were standing, hats on. The smoke and the smell of the barbecue were

already ascending to quicken appetites with suggestions of the feast to come, and preliminary shouts,
cheers for this speaker or that, were making the woods
ring."

We all know how that Fourth of July debate turned
out. Toombs, "with his unlit cigar, his gold-headed
cane, his mass of disordered hair . . . his big black eyes,
which flashed with the joy of battle," was the persuader
who led the state on the course it probably had already
set for itself — secession from the union. But your
heart goes out to the man who later served as vice
president of the Confederacy and spoke against secession — Stephens, "so frail looking, so wan and sad, so
self-possessed and reserved, looking so much like some
old spinster dressed in man's clothing."

The nation surely must have looked like it was going
to hell in a handbasket that Fourth of July. But it didn't.

August

THE OLD ROMAN emperors were certainly high-handed with the calendar. Take August. They treated it like it was their own personal swatch of sweet, warm summertime. Julius Ceasar had a month named for him — July. So nothing would do his successor Augustus but that he honor himself with the next month. He picked it as his lucky month because he had been elected consul and completed the conquest of Egypt then. But there was one little fly in the ointment. His predecessor, Julius Caesar, had himself a thirty-one-day month, while August had only thirty days. No problem for an emperor. He just lifted a day from February, already a short month, and tacked it onto August as if it were a patch on some growing, Roman kid's toga!

A friend of mine who *hates* August can blame Augustus for dragging it out another day.

She says it's a do-nothing month, fit only for the dogs, whose "days" fall in this hottest part of the summer. She believes in turning up the air-conditioning and getting in bed with a supply of books and waiting it out. People in history seem to have done something similar because, except for Columbus' third landing on the American continent in August, 1502, there hasn't been much stirring accomplishment. Even the birthdays aren't times of national rejoicing — Napoleon Bonaparte's in August, 1769 and Francis Scott Key's in August, 1779.

Nevertheless, I love old hot, opulent, sun-ripe August. It's bathing suits drying on the clothesline; the song of the old, salt-stained, ice cream freezer turning custard while we sit late under the maple tree. It's hammock time and the sound a frog makes plopping in the pond when we go swimming. It's riding in the back of the pickup truck, picking blackberries, and canning beans; it's the whisper of fresh-watered hanging baskets dripping under the eaves; the agitated potracking of my neighbor's guineas when they have spotted a snake in the grass.

In the old days, and still in the rural South, crops are "laid by," which is to say there's nothing left to do with cotton and corn and tobacco until the harvest, and families have headed for Old Shiloh or Salem or Smyrna campground for a week of preaching and singing. There are still old wooden "tabernacles" surrounded by little camp shacks where families reunion, eat gargantuan meals, and gain spiritual refreshment at twice-daily revival preaching services. In years gone by, farm families tied the milk cow to the wagon and hauled her along to meeting to make sure of a bountiful sweet milk, buttermilk, and cream supply during meeting. Every campground I have ever visited depended on a spring somewhere down the hill for its water supply, and walking to the spring was a courtship ritual for young couples at the meeting.

Things have changed markedly at these camp grounds. The little camp shacks called "tents" are no longer dirt-floored with sheets strung up on lines to provide what little privacy there was for dressing and sleeping. They have walls and screens instead of net mosquito bars. Electricity provides them with lights and ice and stoves, which are somewhat cooler than the old wood ranges once used for cooking. I even heard of a man who dared to stay away from the evening meeting at the tabernacle after supper. He remained behind to watch a baseball game on a portable television set. I think his wife must have had trouble facing her neighbors on the hard benches in the tabernacle.

The preaching services probably have not changed much, although the Bible has been rewritten to make more understandable but less beautiful the words of the old King James version. The old hymns most certainly have been retained, and the hot August air will reverberate night after night with "Amazing Grace" and that ancient harvest song, "Bringing in the Sheaves."

Sometimes I worry that the day will come when camp meeting will be no more. There is a charming, little town on Martha's Vineyard called Oak Bluffs, which was founded as a meeting spot for Methodists. It has the fine, open-air pavillion in the center with mighty oak trees shading it, but the "tents," far from being primitive shacks, are more like tiny, Victorian houses. Built for the same purpose as ours, they were more weather-tight, a little bigger, and were ornamented with carpenter's lace — the jigsaw folderols which decorated porches and roofs of the eighties and nineties. Today they are widely sought as summer homes for Martha's Vineyard resort people, are painted in delicate ice cream colors, and make the house magazines for their architectural and interior design interest.

It's hard to believe that the people who dwell in those chic, little "tents" open their windows to the hot summer evenings and sing along with the lifted voices in the tabernacle about the "dangers, toils, and snares" which grace led them through.

Celestine Sibley

For many of us, August is a prime vacation month. It is beach-going time. I know a family that has a house on Dog Island off the coast of northwest Florida, and the members take turns using it. My friend, a woman with several children, says there's always spirited competition for the beach house in August.

"Sure it's hot," she says. "The dog flies and mosquitos can be pests. Jellyfish and stingrays come into the beach when you're swimming." She smiled dreamily. "I feel sorry for people who have to be anywhere else."

She is so used to cataloging the drawbacks to her brothers and sisters to gain the house for her family's use that she has come to regard even the irritants as virtues. She dare not mention the blueness of the water, the whiteness of the sand, the music of the surf, the spectacular sunrises and sunsets, the cool gulf breezes, or she would do herself out of August occupancy.

The first person on that magical island to invite us to drop by, when I went down there to finish a book a few years ago, was a woman who grew up in South Georgia and now lives in Pennsylvania.

"Come for a drink," she said. "Around five o'clock."

It sounded ominously like a citified cocktail hour to me, and I hadn't brought along even one dress.

"Mary Ellen," I demurred, "I just brought bluejeans."

She nodded. "Roll 'em up when you wade down the beach to see us," she said matter-of-factly.

We did wade down the beach to her father's house and mounted the steps to a porch looking out on the sunset. She said her husband had gone up the island in the Jeep to pick up a New Orleans doctor and his wife, who were also coming for cocktails. Hmmn, I thought, they'll probably be dressed up. Then I took my eyes off the sunset long enough to behold my host and the other guests pushing the Jeep down deep, sanded ruts of the beach road. We went out to help, and I realized contentedly that Dog Island social life was my kind of social life.

At that time, a couple named Doris and Dewey were the oldest settlers on the island. They looked after things for the then principal owner, the late Jeff Lewis, renting a few little efficiency apartments and running the only near-commercial establishment on the island. It was called The Hut, and you could buy cigarettes and soft drinks there, sometimes beer, a box of salt, or a bottle of ketchup. They had radio communication with the mainland and the boats that plied the waters of St. George sound, and they were a sort of message and social center.

When I was deposited on the island, my family instructed me to touch base with Dewey and Doris every day — so somebody would know that I was alive and well, had not drowned in the surf or been done in by cottonmouth moccasins or rattlesnakes during my rambles across little creeks and through the swamps and pine woods. I made a point of leaving the typewriter at 5 P.M., walking for an hour, and swinging back by The Hut by six o'clock for a drink and a chat with Doris and Dewey. Once I was stuck on a problem, and I admitted to them that my work was going slowly.

"Aw," said Doris, "can we hep you?"

"Don't have no education," put in Dewey. "Never got much chance at school when I was a young'un, so I ain't no book-writer. But if I can hep you, you know I will."

"I know," I said, and then I had an idea. "Dewey, do you know anything about turpentining?"

"Sure do," he said. "Turpentined most of my life."

"Do you know anything about moonshining?"

"Sure do," he said. "Put in some time at that, too."

My problem was how a liquor still might set a woods fire, which would spread to a turpentine still and ignite the barrels of rosin around it with a conflagration so mighty it would fatally burn a man.

Dewey knew exactly and delineated it for me in careful detail. I hurried back to my typewriter.

The next day I dropped by The Hut and sought out Dewey.

"You know anything about Model-T cars?" I asked.

"Sure do," said Dewey. "Know all about 'em."

"Well, if your Model-T was wrecked pretty bad, could you fix it if you lived 'way back in the country where you couldn't get parts?"

"You got any kind of shop?" Dewey asked.

"It's a lumber mill," I said. "They got a blacksmith shop and probably all kinds of machinery around."

"Then you can fix it," said Dewey. "Now, let's see what's broke . . ."

Later I went back with a copy of the finished book inscribed to Dewey and Doris, thanking them for their help. Dewey was reluctant to take it.

"I couldn't hep no book-writer," he protested.

"Dewey, you are as good as the Library of Congress," I told him, and it was true.

Ill-health, the death of Jeff Lewis, and the change of the island's ownership have sent Dewey and Doris ashore to live in a trailer they owned, closer to doctors and hospitals. The Hut no longer has even a bottle of ketchup to sell, but it is still used as a meeting place for property owners. The old store shelves are filled with a library of sorts — the books people bring for vacation reading and donate when they are finished. It's wonderful to be able to swing by there and borrow a murder mystery when you run out of something to read, but as a reference source, that shelf of books can't equal Dewey.

Many colleges have what they call summer commencement this month. Emory University invited my friend the late Dr. Bell Wiley, a Civil War historian, to speak at summer graduation ceremonies the year before he died. Dr. Wiley was one of the best writers and one of the funniest speakers in the region, and I was delighted with his topic: "Southern Women: Tragic Yesterdays, Triumphant Tomorrows."

He had just finished a book on Confederate women at that time, and his talk supplied grist for my continuing battle with people who would present Southern women as sugar-mouthed, lily-handed, vaporous idiots.

Dr. Wiley had evidence that they were meaner than their menfolk in despising and denouncing Yankees at the time of the Civil War. They also served as spies, nurses, worked in ordnance plants and textile mills, and, toughest of all, planted and plowed the fields, reaped the harvests, killed the hogs, cured the meat, cut the firewood, spun and wove their own clothes and cloth for uniforms, tanned leather for shoes, treated illnesses without help of doctors or drugs, and mostly wrote cheerful letters to their men at the front. Sometimes they even wrote funny and racy letters to their husbands, said Dr. Wiley, whose books were based on old letters.

"Romantic writers of the moonlight and magnolia school portray Southern women as refined, ethereal creatures untainted by vulgar thoughts, coarse language, and the attractions of the world — the flesh and the devil," he said. "This concept is not supported by

[93]

primary sources' treating of Confederate women. Rather, these records indicate that Southern women of the late 1860s, while often playing the role of dainty, delicate, high-minded beings, were in reality very much like their great-granddaughters of the present time."

He quoted one lady who said in a letter to her husband that she wanted to be with him so badly she got "the all overs" and a "perfect fever."

"One of the most impressive qualities demonstrated by Confederate women was staunchness in adversity," Dr. Wiley told his audience. "No generation of Southern women experienced anything like the hardship of wives and mothers who were subjected to the ordeal of the blockade, invasion, and defeat in the terrible conflict of the 1860s."

I loved the letter a Virginia woman wrote to her husband:

"Donte be uneasy about us. We will try and take care of ourselves the best we can. I donte minde what I do just so you can get back safe."

You can't tell it from the temperature of late August, but there is a tinge of fall in the air. You might be sweltering, barefooted, and in ragged shorts, but you know in your bones that the season called Almost Autumn is on you.

Twilight is a good time to wander forth, if you live in the country. The heat has lifted, and a small breeze rises somewhere in the pasture. Once there were houses along this road where the pasture is now. They have all been gone for years (since before I came to Sweet

Apple), but they left an imprint on the land — big oaks that once shaded their rooftops; a thicket of old-fashioned, watermelon-pink crepe myrtles; and ragtag remnants of flower gardens.

From the evidence available so far, it is going to be a bountiful autumn. The black walnut tree is loaded with green fruit and so is the persimmon. In the dying light I can't see the muscadines on the wild tangle of vines in the trees, but I am sure they are there. I have seen fallen fruit on the ground.

There will be plenty of maypops, judging from the number of delicate, lavendar flowers — called passion flowers in the seed catalogs — in the fence row.

Down by the creek, the thistles have taken up their stand. Since Leonard Foote, a naturalist, told me years ago that wildflowers move around and you can't count on finding them in the same place every year, I have worried that the pink thistles which grow so profligately by the creek might move to other fields. I have seen it happen to hepaticas and black-eyed Susans and Joe Pye weed. But the thistles stand, deceptively delicate and graceful looking and ready to be cut for a bouquet in the old, rose-painted, cream pitcher . . . when I remember to come armed with gloves and clippers.

The sun is long gone from the road when I climb the last hill toward home. A brown thrasher, out late, swerves swiftly homeward across my path. A whippoorwill sounds in the woods, and from the ditch by the roadside a faint, indefinable fragrance rises. Goldenrod, or is it over-ripe elderberries? I think it might be the smell of August.

September

ALTHOUGH I don't know the real reason the founders of September's great national celebration, Labor Day, picked this month for it, I can sure see why. It's an energetic month. Things start stirring in September. School begins, vacations end, serious projects suddenly engross us. Even hurricanes, which have been slumbering unborn down in the Carribean, start their birth movement, reminding gulf coasters that big winds are brewing.

The scriptures are full of references to labor, beginning with "Six days shalt thy labor" and including the catechism pledge, "To lean and labor truly to get mine own living and to do my duty in that state of life unto which it shall please God to call me." But the United States government didn't pay much attention to the problems of labor until the country was over a hundred years old. In 1884, Congress established a Bureau of Labor in the Department of Interior, waiting four years to give it department status and then blending it with Commerce — the Department of Labor and Commerce. It became an independent Department of Labor in the administration of President Woodrow Wilson in 1913. Meanwhile, laboring people were thinking about it, and in 1882 Peter J. McGuire, founder of the United Brotherhood of Carpenters, suggested a national holiday to honor the country's working people. The campaign for a Labor Day was on. Workers staged parades in New York, but it was the state of Oregon which first made Labor Day a legal holiday. In 1887 President Grover Cleveland came through, signing a bill which made it a national holiday. Other countries by now have adopted Labor Days of their own, although in Australia they call it Eight Hour Day, in commemoration of the successful struggle for a shorter working day.

With Labor Day weekend being the last official piece of time for leisure and fun before winter begins, September is launched into real busy-ness. Now come the autumnal equinox, cool nights, hot days, and harvest time. Our country's founders felt the push of the season. Columbus set sail on September 25, 1493, for his second voyage to America. The Pilgrims nosed the prow of their good ship the Mayflower out of old England and headed toward the rocky coast of New England on September 16, 1620. There were other energetic happenings. Elias Howe patented the sewing machine in 1846, the Germans began the blitz of London in 1940, and the British signed a treaty ending the American Revolution in September, 1783.

In families with children, it is the new shoes and new fall coat month. The weather, of course, can be as yes-and-no as at any time in the year.

Helen Hunt Jackson, the novelist, gave it an accolade:

September days are here,
With summer's best of weather
And autumn's best of cheer.

Maybe so, maybe not. But there is always a day in late September when you are suddenly content to be where you are, doing what you're doing, possibly the only day like that in 365.

One September, that day caught me at 4 A.M. looking for a warm housecoat and last winter's bedroom slippers, both packed away for the summer, naturally. I bundled up anyhow and went out in the backyard to enjoy the waning moonlight while I waited for the coffee. It seemed to me unlikely for the season of the year, but the trees were shivering. The hammock chain creaked coldly under the maple tree in a wind which smelled of hayfields and ripening. Somewhere over toward the river, a hound dog lifted his voice in a mournful paean to the moon.

The day, when it arrived, seemed to me to be as perfect as days come. The sun touched my clothesline, and the faults which my mother would have found in my laundry — grass stains on the knees of britches, sheets less than snowy white — were not visible to me. From a distance, the things drying there were a string of bright banderoles stirring lightly in the amber air.

While you check the hems and seams to see if they're dry, you smell the new-cut grass and watch a hummingbird's progress from pink geranium to red salvia. You sidestep a brilliantly-colored skink sunning on the rock step and stop to watch a monster-sized praying mantis swaying on a milkweed bloom.

It's the season of the year when all the little creatures seem to be stirring about, maybe house-hunting against the arrival of winter. There's the giant spider who greets me from the bottom of the sink every morning. I don't know how he gets in there or why, but he can't climb up its slick sides, so twice I have used the kitchen tongs to put him back on the windowsill, hoping he knows his way out from there. This day I used the tongs to take him outside, and he departed with such alacrity that I thought he might like the feel of the day and the earth, too.

Indoors wasn't bad, either. I enjoyed meal-getting with the cool air making me think of soups and stews, of giant apple cobblers and buttery wedges of corn-bread. And when the meals were eaten and I tackled the cleanup, it seemed to me to be very good work. I held the pewter teapot in my hands for a minute after I had dried it, thinking how pretty it was and how good the first cup of hot tea tastes on a cool afternoon. I even got out the copper polish and rubbed up the little tea kettle, loving the way it gleamed and thinking of the friends who gave it to me.

On such a day, a good housewife would air her blankets and quilts. I thought of how it would be in the mountains with fences full of the old patterns — Step Around the Mountain, Double Wedding Ring, Rose of Sharon. I'd like to go and see, but I thought of it too late. The best I could do was to pick up the Christmas stocking I had started for one of the babies and make a gesture toward autumn's beginning with knit and purl.

September is really too warm a month to set out trees, unless you buy them in cans, of course. I bought a fig tree in a gallon can and lugged it around the yard trying to decide where I would plant it. I had a good feeling about it — a sense of oneness with the earth and all the people who have written about it. For, of course, the fig tree holds an old and respected place in the literature of the world. How would Eve have clothed herself after that disastrous sortie into knowledge and sin if the Garden of Eden had not at least one fig tree?

My little tree, as small as it is, already boasts two figs. It took me awhile to dig a hole for it, but there was promise of rain in the air and I was eager to get it in the ground in time for a good drenching. I hacked away at the hard ground and thought of poor Mother Eve, standing there in Eden in her fig leaf apron, hearing those fateful words: "In sorrow thou shall bring forth children . . . In the sweat of thy face shalt thou eat bread, till thou return unto the ground, for out of it was thou taken for dust thou art and unto dust shall thou return."

There's a theological theory that she got us into our troubles, but maybe we also inherited from her a pleasure in the earth and the necessity of sweating to get our bread. I like digging in the earth, and I bet Eve found in it a consolation for some of those troubles that descended on her.

When Cain and Abel started cutting up — acting like hippies or terrorists or, as we used to call them in a more innocent day, juvenile delinquents — Eve may have watered the fig tree with her tears and then felt better about everything.

"While the earth remaineth," I quoted to myself, "seedtime and harvest, and cold and heat, and summer and winter, and day and night shall not cease."

The Bible thought well of the fig tree. It must have been one of the few trees which reliably grew and bore in that hot and arid land. In the book of Micah, there's a suggestion that owning your own land with a fig tree upon it is a great thing. "They shall sit every man under his vine and under his fig tree." And practically the same thing in Maccabees: "Every man sat under his vine and under his fig tree."

There's an old theory that fig trees flourish only close to houses where they can hear the sound of human voices, raised in conversation and laughter and maybe squabbling too, for all I know. But I'm not going to let any unpleasant words be spoken around my fig tree. Not that I'm superstitious, but there's no need to take a chance.

Celestine Sibley

The rains came about the same time my old friend Ann Waldron arrived from Hightstown, New Jersey, for a visit. She saw my mixing bowls deployed all over the kitchen and in some areas of the back porch to catch the drips from the leaking roof.

"Your house *leaks*!" cried urban Annie.

"Well, sure," I said, "doesn't everybody's?"

Apparently since she moved away from her native Birmingham to Tallahassee to Houston to New Jersey, following her husband who worked for the *New York Times*, she has become unacquainted with the ubiquity of a leaking roof. You can think you have it fixed, but you haven't. In my family, we know you can't patch a roof. Patch it here, it gives way there.

Better, I say out of dark resignation and maybe a touch of superstition, let the leaks alone. Shift the furniture if you must. Buy more mixing bowls, my leak catchers, or, if you are modern like my daughter, more plastic buckets. But don't tamper with those leaks.

In a way, it makes for an interesting exercise. Just when you think you know where it's going to leak and get your mixing bowls arranged, that capricious old roof fools you cold. Instead of drenching the pie safe, the drop attacks the rocking chair. And when you replace the cushions in Muv's old rocker with another mixing bowl, the leak moves over to the corner and starts licking at Mrs. Denver Cox's old blue water bench, which we use to seat children at the kitchen table.

"It never leaks in the beds or the bathroom," I told my friend smugly . . . but then I reached out a hand and surreptitiously knocked on the wood of the meat block.

Ann left and the rains continued, and I got myself a cup of coffee and sat in comparative dryness and listened to the tintinnabulation of the rain in the mixing bowls, trying to figure if the size and timbre of the bowls gave the music its variety. The big bowl went *tink-tink-tink*, the little bowl *naa-naa-naah*, the middle-sized bowl *gnee, gnee*. The wind shifted and so did the rain, and there was a break in the music. The drips had changed course and were now falling on wood with a new and totally different sound. Clarinet? No, woodwinds and wood waters don't sound the same.

After a slight rearranging of the bowls and sloshing the mop around, I went back to my coffee and thinking about leaking roofs. A little cold water never hurt anybody. Besides, think of the music you'd miss if you really could patch a roof. I vow my mixing bowls are playing "Sunny Side of the Street" at this very minute.

This is the season when butterflies are everywhere in the country, looking like airborne flowers as they soar in the golden, late-summer light and hover over fading blossoms and dusty leaves. The goldenrod attracts flocks of sulphur moths, the milkweed the far-flying monarchs.

All kinds of classes are starting this month: adult education courses at the colleges, dancing and drawing and macrame and basket weaving at the public parks. Caught up in the back-to-school mood, I always think I might sign up for aerobics or furniture refinishing or conversational French or brain surgery. I never do. I really would like to go back to school and study biology, so when September comes I can recognize and identify the gloriously-colored flying stock which comes to my backyard.

Celestine Sibley

When I was a sophomore at Murphy High School in Mobile, I didn't properly value biology until we got to the study of butterflies and moths and trees. The teacher had finally found something within my experience (what did I care about amoebas?) and I spent every weekend joyfully prowling the woods, putting names to old friends which had been nameless. If we could have kept our faces out of microscopes and left off the embarrassing discussion about the fertilization of eggs, I might have become a biologist.

Not all the visitors late summer brings to the dooryard are so welcome. I am not perturbed to see the wasps hard at work putting the finishing touches to some gray edifice under the eaves. The honey bees mesmerize me with their sweet humming, and I am amused by the big, pollen-dusted bumble bees tumbling awkwardly around the white spires of the phlox. But there's one fellow who sets me screeching for help: the snake.

We haven't had any snakes this summer. At least I haven't seen any, and I was hoping that Sweet Apple was like Gladys Taber's Stillmeadow — a little living, a little protesting, a little activity with a hoe, and the snakes moved to the tall timber.

Unfortunately, it's not that way. I was dragging the hose across the yard at dusk, and I saw a length which was not hose-green but snake-black. The gentleman who heard my howl for help and came to the rescue recognized that visitor as a friend — a king snake — and deliberately let him get away. To hear him tell it, I'm the luckiest woman alive to have that king snake on the premises. What no man understands is that it matters not if the snake is a whole SWAT team where poisonous snakes are concerned. His sin is being visible. He can have the woodshed, the rock wall, the entire yard, if he'll just stay out of sight. But you can't explain that to a man.

My grandson wrote that he spent his birthday check to buy a dictionary, and I was aglow for days. To give a child the gift of words is better than that other thing he covets — a twenty-foot sailboat. I promptly started planning other books I can send him for Christmas and birthdays and plain no-reason occasions.

Meanwhile, a forty-two-year-old poet wrote enclosing some of his works.

"Do you think I should learn to spell?" he asked. "Is it neccesary (*sic*) to a writer?"

Well, not absolutely "neccesary." The novelist Harry Lee, who worked for our newspaper back in the 1940s, was such a remarkably bad speller that he was the delight of our copy desk. The copy editors hailed each new Harryesque horror in spelling as a triumph of humor bordering on sheer genius. But he could write and had three very good novels published to prove it.

However, correct spelling is desirable, and I'd give it a try, I told the poet. Editors and random correspondents like me will bless you. And I went right out and bought my grandson another dictionary, in case he decides to try his hand at poetry. This one is a rhyming dictionary. If he ever looks for something to rhyme with cue, dew, or ewe, it's all right here: knew, mew, stew, sue, view, yew, adieu, anew, and about twenty more which I certainly wouldn't have thought of — askew, bedew, endue, imbue, mildew, purlieu, and even interview, revenue, and finally, Jew.

Celestine Sibley

She's been silent a long time, my favorite cur-
mudgeon and nag. I haven't had a letter from her
poking fun at my pleasure in country living since they
turned the old apartment building, where she has lived
for many years, into a condominium. I feared that she
had been driven to the sticks, a locale she despises and
deplores.

But no, she is still a flower of sidewalks and street
lights. And still a nag.

"Tell me, dear one," she wrote, "what do you
bucolic bumpkins do when the sun goes down and you
can't rush around effusing over flower and tree?"

It was on the tip of my typewriter to tell her that most
of us country bumpkins do what her city types do — go
indoors and watch the news and then fall asleep over a
book.

Happily, there are other things we country people
also do, but I was reluctant to tell her. Until it is pitch-
black dark, we sit in the backyard and watch the moonflowers open. It is one of the pleasantest things anybody can do as the sun goes down and darkness comes
to the earth. If you don't have moonflowers, put them
on your list when you dispatch your garden and flower
seed order next spring. Edith Henderson, the landscape architect, suggested them to me — trained over a
rustic trellis to screen the terrace from the road.

We planted them and we have replanted them almost
every spring since — a continuing summer show. We
gather at twilight to watch the great, white, fragrant
blossoms, one after another, gently and delicately
unfold their satin petals, which are subtly marked with
pale green veins.

My friend will not concede that moonflowers will
ever replace street lights, but it's a pretty exciting end-
of-the-day pageant to us. A whippoorwill tunes up
back in the woods, there's a symphony of cicadas in the

maple trees, the sweet scent of watered grass rises from the earth, and we hitch our chairs closer to the fence and call out, "Look! Ah, watch that one! There's another one!"

Perhaps I'm thinking more of moonflowers than of September's big celebration, Labor Day, when I go indoors thinking of the Psalmist's petition: "Prosper thou the work of our hands upon us, O prosper thou our handy-work."

October

A MAN I KNOW who has lived in England for many years used to plan his annual trip back to the United States for October.

"There's no place as beautiful as Georgia in October," he said.

"You mean it's prettier than England?" I said, surprised. I once spent two weeks in England in October, and I thought it was a season and a country of matchless beauty.

"I don't know," he admitted sheepishly. "I've never been able to stay away from Georgia in October."

Another friend, listening to this exchange, nodded sagely. "Like I've always said, there's no place October doesn't become."

It is a *becoming* month, one that the heat-weary old world would be lucky to wear more often. People who must have had some of our current passion for numbers named it October for eight, the then eighth month in the Roman calendar. After the calendar got changed around, there was a movement afoot to change old Eight's name to Antoninus for a Roman emperor or Faustinus for his wife. Even the historian Tacitus was thought of as somebody to name a month for, but the people liked October and steadfastly refused to use any of the new names. (Would that Atlantans would do

[109]

likewise, when the city plays fast and loose with old family names, dropping them and substituting the name of a more recent hero or notion. I find International Boulevard particularly repugnant as a substitute for honest old Cain Street, but Atlantans, unlike Romans, are abundantly accepting of change.)

It must have been very pleasant for Christopher Columbus to first behold the New World on October 12, 1492. School children, and particularly Italian segments of the population, celebrate that anniversary, but the day passes without any particular sentiment for most of us.

And yet old Christopher was a hero worth remembering and honoring. In this space age, with the unknown analyzed and documented and explored, we forget what courage it must have taken for that son of a Genoa wool-comber to take his three, frail ships and strike out across "The Sea of Darkness," as the Atlantic ocean was then called. He believed in his voyage so strongly that he had persuaded his Catholic priest and, through him, Queen Isabella of Spain to believe too and to help him. But his crew were ordinary seaman of little vision, and they were terrified of the horrible monsters which were said to inhabit the ocean. They must have grown weary of the two-month voyage, probably with little water and wormy food. I thought of them recently when I saw on television a rerun of *Mutiny on the Bounty*. Columbus' crew also threatented mutiny, I have read, but like Captain Bligh, Christopher was an indominatible fellow at the helm of a ship. Somewhere on this day, school children will recite the Joaquin Miller poem which celebrates that:

> *Behind him lay the gray Azores,*
> *Behind the Gates of Hercules;*
> *Before him not the ghost of shores,*
> *Before him only shoreless seas.*

The good mate said: "Now we must pray,
For lo! the very stars are gone.
Brave admiral, speak, what shall I say?"
"Why, say, 'Sail on! Sail on! Sail on!'"

Joaquin Miller moralized a bit when he got to that
sight of land on October 12. It grew to be, he wrote,
"Time's burst of dawn." And of the Admiral;

He gained a world; he gave that world
Its grandest lesson: "On! Sail on!"

October may not have been Columbus' birthday. I
never saw a month mentioned, and of the year, the
books say "probably 1451." But a lot of other famous
people saw the light of day in this lovely month: President Dwight Eisenhower (1890); the aviator Eddie
Rickenbacker (1890); Mohandas Ghandi (1869), the
Indian political leader; Cordell Hull (1871), the Tennessee statesman; Geoffrey Chaucer (1340), the English
poet; President Theodore Roosevelt (1858); poet John
Keats (1795); the scientist Jonas Salk (1914). The first
Model-T Ford was built on October 1, 1908; the cor-
nerstone of the White House was laid on October 13,
1792; and "the blackest day in stock market history,"
the crash which precipitated the Great Depression,
occurred on October 29, 1929. We don't pay much
attention to the natal day of our President's wives, but I
bet many people whose lives were touched by her in
one way or another remember that Eleanor Roosevelt
was an October child — October 11, to be exact.

Mrs. Roosevelt was a heroine to me. Her plainness,
her simplicity, her common sense moved me. I think if
she had been a young beauty who made the Best
Dressed lists and gave chic parties, I might not have
been so drawn to her. But she was an awkward girl, a

homely woman who had almost no vanity, no apparent egoism. She was shy but overcame it to go out into the world to be her crippled husband's strong legs, his eyes and his ears, and, in some instances, I believe, his conscience. She worried about ignorance and poverty. She fought racism, and frankly she nagged her husband about the need for women in government.

"I might go to my husband and say that I was very weary of reminding him to remind the members of his cabinet and his advisers that women were in existence," she wrote in 1949, "that they were a factor in the life of the nation and increasingly important politically."

Sometimes he listened to her. Sometimes he asked for suggestions. Sometimes he didn't. But she didn't let up on what she believed in. She was tactful, she was gracious, but she was also outspoken, and her interest and sympathies knew no bounds.

Once I sat next to her on a platform at the old Wesley Memorial church downtown. I remember wishing, as I hastily dressed that morning, that I had time to prepare a proper speech. But I didn't worry that I didn't have time to take a turpentine and rag to the paint splatters on my arms, because the morning was cool and I was wearing a covering suit coat. Mrs. Roosevelt herself didn't awe me. I don't know if other First Ladies at that time would have moved around so freely with no Secret Service escort, no entourage, but Mrs. Roosevelt walked in alone in her common-sense shoes and her funny old hat, carrying a knitting bag, looking like any church-going grandmother. She was easy and comfortable to sit with. As the morning progressed, the weather grew warmer, and I thoughtlessly took off my suit jacket, forgetting my paint smears. I hung the coat on the back of my chair and looked around to see Mrs. Roosevelt examining my splotched arms with considerable interest.

Flustered, I said hurriedly, "I'm trying to fix up an apartment to rent in my basement. I was painting there until late last night and I didn't have time . . ."

"Well, now these are very pretty colors," said Mrs. Roosevelt. "This green . . . what are you painting green?"

Woodwork in the livingroom, I told her.

"And the wall?" she asked.

She went down my arms and wrists like they were a color card, pointing and asking and approving the combinations. She really seemed to care that I make a success of that project, and later I understood why. She was often trying to fix up a cottage or an apartment herself.

Several years after President Roosevelt died, Mrs. Roosevelt came back to Georgia for a day's visit. Hugh Stovall, the newspaper photographer, and I went out to the home of her Atlanta friends, Mr. and Mrs. Charles Palmer, to have coffee with her and to follow her to Warm Springs. She had to have been an old woman then, but she was absolutely tireless. She went at a dead run all day long, visiting patients and staff at the Warm Springs hospital, stopping to speak to every person. She went back to the Little White House and talked with the people who were keeping it open as a museum and walked quietly though the simple, unpretentious rooms, pausing for a moment in the one where her husband had died. Afterwards, she went out on the mountainside to a bluff overlooking the valley, where President Roosevelt had liked to cook out and there had many family picnics.

As she got out of the car and walked over to the precipice, Stovie reached for his camera. And then, looking at the lonely old lady standing silhouetted against the fading sunset, he slowly put it back. We both felt it was a moment when a woman who didn't even ask for it deserved privacy.

Years later on a trip of Mexico City, I took along the biography *Eleanor and Franklin*, which Joseph P. Lash wrote. I came to the President's death one night when I had let friends go off to dinner without me. I was alone when I read of the presence of Lucy Mercer, his long-time love, at the Roosevelt cottage when the President died. Mrs. Roosevelt had not known she was there, and her pain and humiliation must have been insupportable when she found out. Sitting there alone in a strange city, I wept for the gallant woman I had known only slightly.

As far as I know, Mrs. Roosevelt never referred to the Lucy Mercer affair, certainly not publicly. But I reread her book, *This I Remember*, not long ago, and I came on some lines which may or may not have applied. She spoke of schooling herself to accept the possibility that some or all of her sons might be killed in World War II, and that her husband could be killed or die at any time.

"This was not consciously phrased," she wrote. "It simply underlay all my thoughts and merged what might happen to me with what was happening to all the suffering people of the world. That does not entirely account for my feelings, however. Perhaps it was that much further back I had had to face certain difficulties until I decided to accept the fact that a man must be what he is, life must be lived as it is . . . you can not live at all if you do not learn to adapt yourself to your life as it happens to be."

Protestant children who grow up in Catholic cities like Mobile, New Orleans, and Pensacola always have the feeling that their Catholic friends have a distinct advantage — all those saints, statues, innumerable feasts days. All Saints Day, uniquely coupled with its lively and pagan eve, Halloween, is an example. We had no personal celebration of All Saints' Day, so we depended on our Catholic friends to invite us along when they went to the cemetery on October 30, to clean and decorate the graves of their relatives and friends, and to special masses on October 31, to pray for them and all the saints of the church. My remembrance of Halloween — or All Hallows Eve, as it is properly called — of those days is fragrant smoke rising in small, delicate, blue-gray columns from many little leaf fires in the cemetery as the grave lots were raked and swept, and the pungent smell of chrysanthemums, one of the few flowers to survive early frost which therefore were placed on the graves and used to decorate the grass.

It was a placid, almost reverent occupation for a day which is also feast day of all those things the Christian church has opposed over the centuries — witches, goblins, fairies, and auguries. How this curious mixture of the religious and the secular came about is one of the mysteries of human celebration. We do know that Pope Gregory IV placed All Saints Day in the church calendar in the ninth century as a sort of roundup of saints since there were more of them than there were days in the year. But he most certainly was opposed to all the spooky, supernatural stuff that has made Halloween fearful and funny and full of fortune-telling gambits through the ages. Would the good pope have told the people that the spirits of the dead wander abroad on All Hallows Eve and join the company of devils and witches and mischief-making elves? Probably not.

Actually, Americans — predominantly Protestant —

didn't pay much attention to either All Saints Day or Halloween until 1840, when the Irish came swarming in to escape the potato famine. They brought with them both the religious celebration and the folklore about witches and cats and nocturnal, evil shenanigans. The jack-o'-lantern is an Irish invention and a splendid one.

When the little boys in our family clamor to stop by the roadside and buy big pumpkins, and when they risk life and limb with their father's knives trying to outdo one another with carving great, grinning faces, I carefully refrain from telling them about Jack. When they are older, they can know that he was, the legend goes, an Irish lad who was bad to sin, worse to drink, and very stingy. He bested the devil in several deals, so when it came time for Jack to die, he couldn't go to heaven because of his sins and the devil wouldn't have him, either. The only thing he could wangle from old Satan was one coal of fire, which he used to light his way into the dark night.

He didn't have a pumpkin handy, so he scooped out a turnip and put the coal inside, making it a lantern. Poor fellow, he is condemned to walk the earth until Judgment Day with that puny lantern.

Trick-or-treating has an uncertain history. In many countries, it was a night when people begged pennies for various church and charity enterprises. Nuts and apples have always been a Halloween staple because they are in season, and for many years that's what people gave children. The switch to collecting for UNICEF, now widely popular and a great relief to our family, was started in Philadelphia in 1950 when some Sunday school children sent in to UNICEF headquarters $17 they had collected trick-or-treating. We like it because it makes even little fellows mindful of children who are hungry and in need of medicine, and it saves them tummy aches from too many indigestible goodies too late in the evening — not to mention the recent unspeakable threat that sick-minded people will give them something that could hurt them.

The only thing most women I know find wrong with October is that it is the month when a nice game, a form of vigorous exercise, suddenly becomes a mind-enslaving, body-paralyzing form of madness, infecting the nation. They hate to see the men in their families go crazy, writhing and howling in front of television sets. They hate to see the food they cooked hurriedly, heedlessly gobbled or rejected entirely. They are confused by the language, the talk of downs and passes and bootleg plays, none of which sounds really nice. They chafe at the lonely times when they have no one to talk to and no one to be with. But this being October, they brace themselves against an invincible adversary. What it is, of course, is football.

Now, I am one of those who doesn't really mind football . . . if I can get out of the house and go to the game, that is. It's like opera. I don't understand the words, but the music is pleasant, the color and the atmosphere beguiling. I like to look at the people and the costumes, the pretty little cheerleaders, the smart officials with their incomprehensible gestures. I love the bands and the high-stepping majorettes and the raucous involvement of the people around me. When I was a child visiting relatives in a little town in northwest Florida, I undertook to learn the deaf mute alphabet and some sign language to be able to converse with a delightful woman who was born deaf. It was a triumph for a child to be able to understand her signs, but I wasn't as subject to untoward merriment then as I am now. These days when an official in short pants stands up before 100,000 people and gestures straight-armed, straight-handed toward his heart, I am convulsed to learn he is saying *Illegal motion*. I fall out laughing when he grasps his wrist with one hand and, translated, has said *Illegal use of hands*, and a roar of anger or agony goes up from the crowd. At times like these, I am prone to agree with an old mountain man who looked across his cornfield fence at kids running and falling and piling on one another, all for the possession of a totally uninteresting little ball.

"That thar footbal," he said, "is a sight. Don't plant no pertaters but it keeps 'em out devilment."

The boys in my family think I should make an effort to get the hang of *first downs*, for instance. They regard me as pretty stupid to be so literal-minded about *conversions*. The only way I grasp the game at all is to inquire into its history. Did you know, I say conversationally, usually during a commercial, that Princeton and Rutgers played the first football game in 1869? Did you know that Harvard players didn't *run* with the ball until they learned about it from Canada's McGill University team in 1874? They didn't know . . . or couldn't answer because their mouths were full of the meal they neglected for a solid half.

But at least I've had my say and am free to leave football and go rake leaves.

The poet Edgar Allan Poe was such a melancholy fellow that he had winter coming prematurely in October:

The skies they were ashen and sober;
The leaves they were crisped and sere —
The leaves they were withering and sere;
It was a night in the lonesome October
Of my most immemorial year.

The poem is "Ulalume," of course, but I don't know what locale Mr. Poe had in mind, because the leaves are at their flamboyant best in most of the country now. North Georgia mountains draw thousands of tourists through the Blue Ridge trails to see the kaleidoscopic foliage. There's no happier outing than a picnic lunch beside a waterfall in the hill country. It's still warm enough, usually, for the children to wade and to hop from rock to rock across tumbling, mountain streams. The air, not the leaves, is crisp, the sky is blue, and the maples and oaks and sourwoods and sweetgums are so brilliant they take your breath away.

Twenty years ago, there were few arts and crafts shows in these parts, until a group up on the Tennessee border started hanging their pictures on a clothesline stretched behind their teacher's studio on the side of a mountain. It was called the Plum Nelly Art Show because it was "plum out of Tennessee and nelly out of Georgia." And it was a hit. From a handful of artists and their friends, it grew to include thousands of trippers out to see the autumnal foliage and ready for any fete. Church groups came and sold refreshments. Men's clubs cleared and levelled fields and organized parking. Weavers and potters and jewelry makers brought their wares. Artists who had found no market for their works discovered that under the spell of the place and the season, the market came to them.

Now, of course, such shows abound. Georgians go to Alabama to buy quilts and swap hound dogs and bring home herbs and pottery. Alabamians go to Ten-

[119]

nessee and Tennessians step over into the Carolinas to pick up a watercolor for the living room or a white oak basket or handwoven rug. It's not that we can't find the handiwork we seek closer to home; it's October. We want to see the asters blooming along the Blue Ridge Parkway or the blaze of sumac against the gray, granite cliff in Mulberry Gap. It's wonderful to be abroad in the land and better if you can bring home a little keepsake to remind you when the skies are indeed "ashen and sober" and the leaves have become "crisped and sere" of October's glories.

November

IN OUR FAMILY we feel so strongly about one of November's principal events — Election Day — that my daughter almost called off the birth of her second son, Ted, because it conflicted with voting. "Mother will never speak to me if I don't get to the polls!" she gasped between labor pains on her way to the hospital.

She didn't vote that day, and I have given up reminding her of it since Ted is now of voting age himself. Two votes, where there was one, quite compensates for that dereliction on November 3, 1964.

Nothing short of a new baby in the family excuses failure to exercise that franchise, of course. When I was a child in the country in South Alabama, people had to pay a poll tax for the privilege of voting, and even the poorest somehow managed to raise that sum and got to the voting place, even if they had to walk miles through a rain storm to get there. Many times children were excused from absence from the two-room Creola school because the ponds had risen and they couldn't cross them. But on election day, their parents wanted no excuse. They got there if they had to wade, swim, or press a leaky rowboat into service.

My father, who sometimes served as an election official, bragged that there were twenty-four voters in the precinct — twenty-three Democrats and a Republican

[123]

— and twenty-four votes were dependably cast. The privilege of casting a vote was precious to those people, because most of them had heard the stories of their ancestors who were disfranchised for service in the Confederate Army or had migrated from countries across the sea where they had no say in the government. I don't believe anybody was ever heard to remark cynically that one vote wouldn't make any difference. Every vote counted, every vote was of equal value. Election Day was as American as that other November celebration — Thanksgiving Day — and as suspenseful as a football game and sometimes as bloody as a shooting war.

As a teen-age reporter working part-time for *The Mobile Press*, I caught the infection of covering election night when Franklin D. Roosevelt won his first landslide victory. The paper occupied an old church building on St. Michael Street in those days, along with an auto parts store and some other enterprises which were built onto or into the thick walls of the old sanctuary. As the youngest and least experienced hand available, I was assigned to take returns over the auto parts store's telephone, which had been borrowed for the occasion. The excitement was in the newsroom, of course, since the national returns poured in there. The AP teletype machines clacked out those from all over the country. And as fast as they came in, they were flashed onto a screen on a building across the way. Crowds milled about the street, watching and cheering. Meanwhile, it was very quiet in the auto parts store. My phone was the last to be rung, only when all others were busy. Finally somebody brought me word that I could leave my post and join the throng on the roof of an adjacent building, watching the dark-lettered slides spell out victory for Mr. Roosevelt on the white sheet across the street. By the time I got there, a victory celebration was in full swing and a torchlight parade was strutting down the street to the music of not one but several bands playing "Happy Days Are Here Again."

It seemed to me then — and I suppose ever since — that those old enough to vote and bring about an event so personal and so vital as choosing a president were enormously lucky.

There have been many election nights since then, all of them exciting, some of them terribly moving. I have sat up with the defeated almost as often as with the victorious. I have been out on the campaign trail with candidates and to polling places where votes were being counted by weary but excited election officials. Once in the mountains, I was looking for the vote counters in a remote cove and was told that they had taken the votes down on the river bank to count them.

"They always count them on the river bank," a friend told me. "All six of them."

There are many more voters in that precinct now, and they no longer take the ballot box to the river bank to examine its urgent contents by the illumination of moonlight and moonshine. Nor is the newspaper the center of returns-gathering any longer. Time was when so many people trooped into the newsroom to see how the election was going that they had to rope off an area where the reporters and editors could work uninterrupted. Candidates and their wives and children came in to make their victory statements and sometimes to grin bravely and concede defeat. Campaign workers and random voters milled about. We drank bad coffee out of paper cups and fought fatigue sometimes until dawn, and it seemed major and history-making.

Now computers have taken over the tabulation of votes, which the wizards from our bookkeeping department once handled. And television stations dispense them, so there are no longer eager crowds standing shoulder to shoulder in the streets with up-lifted faces, waiting suspensefully. You can roll up your hair and put cold cream on your face and get in bed and learn how it's going.

But it's still exciting, that "first Tuesday after the first Monday in November of every even-numbered year."

It is perhaps ironic that the least rememberable Presidents we have elected were born in November — Warren G. Harding (1865) and James A. Garfield (1831) in Ohio, James K. Polk (1795) in South Carolina, Franklin Pierce (1804) in New Jersey, and Zachary Taylor (1784) in Virginia. So were Will Rogers (1879), the humorist; John Philip Sousa (1854), the bandmaster; Madame Marie Curie (1867), the physicist; Charles de Gaulle (1890), the French statesman; and Joe DiMaggio (1914) of baseball fame. It was also a good month for writers to arrive — the Russians Ivan Turgenev (1818) and Feodor M. Dostoevski (1821); Scotsman Robert Louis Stevenson (1850); the Americans Mark Twain (1835) and Louisa M. Alcott (1833). Winston Churchill was born on the last day of the month (1874) and Abraham Lincoln delivered the Gettysburg address on the 19th in 1863.

The trees are bare now, the sky chill and drear. That's why when I got out of the car in my backyard the other night, I saw a streak of light through the woods and turned to learn it was a car on the paved road — the first time I have been able to see that, although the road is fairly close. It was zipping along as if it owned the earth and in full view of my own secluded, tree-enclosed patch. I felt exactly as if I had seen a UFO.

The next morning I saw some men tying Merthiolate-colored paper ribbons to bushes and driving stobs in the ground, and I knew at a glance what they were up to — a survey team marking off land to be sold, bulldozed, and developed. Once more I felt like the old mountain woman who saw smoke from a chimney across the valley and called to her man, "Pa, we jes' as well be moving on. Hit's gittin' too scrouged here."

I think I must know how Wash Collier felt. He had him a business at Five Points in downtown Atlanta, but his farm home was 'way out in the country — near-neighbor to deer and squirrels and raccoons and 'possums and surrounded by beautiful woods. Atlanta grew out and enveloped him with streets and houses, now called Ansley Park and Sherwood Forest. And poor Hardy Ivy, dwelling peacefully in that log cabin on what became Ivy Street . . . how did he feel about the stores and hotels and restaurants that surrounded his little farm?

The trouble is that you can't count on having country very long anymore, and there's no use being greedy about it. It's the nature of city people who moved to the country to think it all belongs to them: I own everything my eye surveys — the pastures and the creek bottoms, the woods and the road to the river. I love it, so I must own it.

But of course that is not true. I own very little beyond today's patch of blue sky, tonight's quietude. There were people before me who waded in the creek — and stilled a little moonshine there — and gathered muscadines in the fall. They knew and loved the shape of the earth, the scent of the morning, and they either died or moved on, leaving the land to those of us who were to come along acting like we'd invented it.

Seeing that car hurtling along the paved road jolted me. I never realized the road was that close or the woods that thin. Seeing the survey crew scared me. But it'll be all right. Maybe nobody will buy the land. And if they do, maybe they won't pave the road or cut down any of the trees.

The difference between me and that mountain woman who knew when she was "scrouged" is that I'm a fool optimist.

It's no longer officially Armistice Day, November 11. The Congress and President Eisenhower changed it to Veterans Day, honoring the servicemen of all wars, in 1954. Some of us still call it Armistice Day, of course, liking the sound of the word, but I looked it up recently and its meaning isn't all that desirable. It means a *temporary* cessation of hostilities by agreement of the warring nations.

That is obviously what we have had — a very temporary cessation — since that first Armistice Day in 1918. But ah, how the people of the world pinned their hopes on its permanence!

The most unforgivable act in time of war is that even after a nation knows it is beaten and is ready to surrender, the shooting goes on. One of the best war movies ever made was *All Quiet on the Western Front*, a story about German soldiers in World War I. Although I haven't seen it in twenty-five or thirty years, I remember vividly the final scene of the movie where the young German, played by Lew Ayres — the only survivor of a group of seven of his classmates — waits out the armistice in the trenches. It is very quiet, and a butterfly lights near the edge of his trench. The boy sees the bright-winged creature and reaches out a trembling hand for it. The quiet is broken by an explosion, and the young hand is still.

This, as I recall, was after the armistice. But in any case, negotiations had been going on for many months. The German High Command had concluded that it couldn't win and had been exchanging letters about the conditions of surrender with the Allies since August. In his book, on which the movie was based, Erich Maria Remarque reported the day-to-day hopes of the young Germans. One by one, the classmates are killed.

There was Detering, a young farmer who kept to himself. "His misfortune was that he saw a cherry tree in a garden," said Paul (Remarque). Knowing that cherry trees were blooming back home, Detering broke a branch and took it with him to his bunk. The next morning he was missing.

"Anyone might have known that his flight was only homesickness and a momentary aberration," wrote Paul. "But what does a court-martial a hundred miles way behind the front line know about it? We have heard nothing more of Detering."

The depression of the young soldiers grew as the food and ammunition supplies diminished. They felt themselves to be "weary, broken, burnt out, rootless, and without hope."

In October 1918, Paul recorded, "Here the trees show gay and golden, the berries of the rowan stand red among the leaves. Country roads run white out to the sky line, and the canteen hums like beehives with rumors of peace."

The closing lines of the book tell us that Paul fell "on a

[129]

day that was so quiet and still on the whole front that the army report confined itself to the single sentence: All quiet on the Western Front."

It must happen in all wars to the armies of all nations. And as we honor the men who fell in that war, the second global war which followed it, Korea, and Vietnam, we can on November 11 but echo the hope President Lyndon Johnson expressed on the fiftieth anniversary of Armistice Day in 1968 — that the day will come "when all the guns of battle will be stilled" forever.

A few months ago I ran out of things to read at the beach, and I started casing the shelves of the people whose cottage we had rented. The husband's interest was clearly technical, the wife's gothic romances. But stuck in the middle of the bosomy paperback jackets was a copy of *A Tale of Two Cities*, which I had not read since I was eleven. That's too young for Dickens and I'm glad, because rereading it seemed a new experience. It kept me going for the rest of the time at the beach, the trip home, and a day or two more. It also set me off on a Dickens kick which I have enjoyed thoroughly.

One of the small pleasures in *A Tale of Two Cities* was meeting again that cold-eyed Frenchwoman, Madame DeFarge, who committed to wool stockinette the intrigue leading to the French revolution and then knit and purled diligently as the tumbrel rolled and the guillotine fell.

I, too, am a knitter. Not a skilled one, certainly not one who could stick to my needles and yarn while the gentry was being beheaded and the blood spurted. But it interests me, soothes me, makes me feel productively employed in those odd snatches of time when I'm riding a bus or a plane, waiting for the bread to rise, or visiting with a friend by the fire in November. They tell me that my great-grandmother knitted and knitted and knitted when her boys were off fighting the Civil War. They marched all over Tennessee and Mississippi in the socks she knitted, and when she ran out of wool, she unraveled the underskirts she had knitted for her daughters and started over again.

A reader named Regina Sabia, clearly a knitter herself, sent me an old book called *Victorian Fancywork*, which extols the value of knitting, embroidery, and crochet for women in all walks of life. "I have often pitied men . . . because they are bereft of our greatest comfort, needlework," says the author. "We get into a kind of fever doing nothing. A very wise country clergyman allowed the women to knit during his sermons. Never had a preacher more attentive listeners; not one of them dropped asleep, as overworked women are apt to do when they for once sit down."

So prodigious a knitter was Eleanor Roosevelt that part of the big Hyde Park Museum on the Hudson River has a section devoted to it. There are the old pictures of her knitting on the campaign trail, on the back platform of trains, at Democratic conventions, in the library at Hyde Park, and, I think, although I do not remember for sure, at the United Nations. The cases show some of her sweaters and a well-worn collection of the old bone needles, which are collectibles in this day of plastic.

Somehow I felt special rapport with her the day I went there with my daughter and granddaughter and stood before that case. Women knit, one of our copy editors wrote, to keep from unraveling. There must have been many times when she felt that necessity.

In any case, when the long, winter evenings of November are upon us and an oak or hickory log stirs on the hearth, breaking red-gold at the heart, a cap for a boy, a sweater for a baby, or a scarf for a friend are all comfortable — and comforting — to hold and to shape under the soothing click of the needles.

We like to call Thanksgiving the oldest and most truly American of our national holidays. Actually, the Book of Judges reports that the Canaanites "went out into the field and gathered their vineyards and trod the grapes and held festival and went to the house of their God and did eat and drink." The Romans held a harvest festival called Cerelia for Ceres, their goddess of grain. They also feasted and drank and danced.

The English celebrated Harvest Home, when the last load of grain was hauled from the field, with singing and merrymaking and, naturally, a big supper.

Even the Cherokee Indians had their Thanksgiving — a four-day fete featuring the green corn dance with rites of purification, during which the whole village was cleansed and renewed. All old clothes and provisions were discarded, new fires were kindled, and the year began afresh while they feasted on new corn.

Elias Boudinot, known to Georgians as a New Englander who came south and lived with the Indians at New Echota just before the infamous Trail of Tears, when they were robbed of their lands and banished to Oklahoma, was the son of a man who first proposed making the Pilgrims' little party a continuing national celebration. A member of Congress from New York, the elder Boudinot proposed a national Thanksgiving in 1789 to thank God "for the many signal favors . . . especially by affording them (the American people) an opportunity peaceably to establish a Constitution of government for their safety and happiness."

Strangely, there was opposition from — of all people — Thomas Jefferson. He called it a "monarchical practice" and ignored the celebration during his eight years in office.

The persistence of a woman — a journalist yet — brought about the holiday as we know it. Mrs. Sarah Josepha Hale, a novelist and editor of *Godey's Lady's Book* of Philadelphia, waged a campaign for Thanksgiving. Abraham Lincoln proclaimed it in 1863, the first time since George Washington had done so in 1789. He chose the last Thursday in November, which prevailed until 1939 when President Franklin D. Roosevelt won the enmity of many of the people who were not already angered by his innovations by moving it to the third Thursday. The country was divided and so vociferously that after two years the President agreed to put the holiday back in its old place — the fourth Thursday in November.

And so it continues today, one of the best of our national observances. It is a long holiday for school children. College students come home. Families reunion. A great deal of cooking goes on. Even in times of privation, families feel some compulsion to bring out their best for Thanksgiving. During the Depression, my mother once made dumplings to go with Vienna sausage for Thanksgiving dinner. She told me often that her grandmother, who presumably had vegetables and some hog meat since they lived on a South Georgia farm, did a lot with sweet potatoes "because grandma had more sweet potatoes than anything else." (I cherish her recipes for sweet potato pone and sweet potato pie, and I wish I had the one for her persimmon beer and persimmon bread.) She was in the same boat with a New Englander who wrote,

We have pumpkins at morning
And pumpkins at noon.
If it were not for pumpkins
We should be undone.

One of my favorite Thanksgiving rites was the Thursday morning service at our old church, North Avenue Presbyterian, where we were members when we lived in Atlanta and the children were growing up. It was held then in the Sunday school rooms with the sun streaming through the windows and only a piano to accompany the singing. The minister read the proclamation of Governor William Bradford of the Plymouth colony setting aside a day to thank God for the bountiful summer harvest, which brought hope and rejoicing to the colonists after the terrible winter of 1620, when about half their number died. There was some scripture reading and a lot of singing of such old-fashioned hymns as "Amazing Grace" and "Old Time Religion," and one I loved "Come ye thankful people come, Raise the song of harvest home." I liked the words, "All is safely gathered in, Ere the winter storms begin." It may not have been true in all our families, but it had a wonderfully comforting sound.

But the best part of the service was a very old-fashioned one for Presbyterians, generally a rather say-nothing, reserved lot. They gave thankfulness testimony. One at a time people who had sat silently in the sanctuary the rest of the year got to their feet and told what they were thankful for. Old people, children, the middle-aged, visitors, revealed their most intimate feelings. I remember that during the war, they spoke haltingly of gratitude for the safety of a husband or son overseas. Sometimes they were thankful for so little as a letter from them.

Before the service ended, a list of those who had died during the year was read, and thanks were said for the lives they had lived and the good they had done. It was done with cheerfulness, even joy, and I have always been thankful for what it showed me — that gratitude for a loved one who lived is much better than grief for his death.

I no longer go to North Avenue's Thanksgiving service. If we can make it, we like to spend the weekend on Dog Island, where the beach goldenrod is a sea of pure gold and the monarch butterflies pause on their migration across the gulf to feast on the abundant pollen. All the children who can go with us, but dinner is easy. It is the custom of Dog Islanders to "put dinner together" up at The Hut, bringing their pies and cakes and salads and covered dishes and setting them out on long tables in the old store building. Someone usually brings a gallon of oysters. There's shrimp and fish, and sometimes youngsters contribute half a keg of beer. The women stir around, setting up the big coffee pot and dispensing paper plates, and we sit at picnic tables on the screened porch or mill around the big room exchanging news of the year. Occasionally, we peer through the big windows at visitors from the north paddling in the surf, and we watch and marvel at their hardihood or foolishness.

There's no religious service beyond a blessing asked by one of our number, but the habit of "counting our thankfuls," as the children used to say, is probably very strong in all of us. And some of us recite inwardly the lines from the Psalm: "O give thanks unto the Lord, for he is good; for his mercy endureth forever."

December

S OME OLD POET whose name I have forgotten fell to early in December and devoted many lines to looking *back* at the year. As I recall, his verse began,

Goodbye kind year, we walk no more together.

We're unusual if we can spend any time at all looking over our shoulder as this month begins. Our compulsion in December, if not as early as Halloween, is to look right under our noses at Christmas. And yet it's a regular month with as much history as any other. It gets its name *decem* from the Latin for ten because it used to be the tenth month in the ancient Roman calendar. March was the first.

"Later," says an old writer, "when two months were added, the numerical significance of its name had been somewhat lost sight of; at any rate, no learned Roman thought it of enough importance to call for a correction."

To further confuse, Caesar even added two days to December, making it a long thirty-one-day month instead of a short twenty-nine-day one.

And a lot of things besides what we regard as its reason for being — Christmas — have occurred in this month. Joel Chandler Harris, the Georgia author of the "Uncle Remus" stories and squire of that old land-mark house in Atlanta's West End, the Wren's Nest, was born on December 9, 1848. John Milton, the English poet, was born on the same day in 1608. James Oglethorpe, founder of Georgia, on December 22, 1696; Joseph Stalin, the Russian dictator, on December 21, 1879; President Woodrow Wilson, December 28, 1856; Kit Carson, the western scout, December 24, 1809; and Walt Disney, December 5, 1901. They repealed Prohibition (1933), founded Phi Beta Kappa (1776) and the American Federation of Labor (1886), ratified the ten amendments of the Bill of Rights (1791), and admitted both Alabama (1819) and Texas (1845) to the union — all in December.

Oh, it has been a month of achievement, one way or another, but oddly enough the birthday most cele-brated in December, that of Jesus Christ, probably did not occur in this month at all. Scholars do not know the exact date of Christ's birth. The observance was shifted around for about three hundred years, and then in A.D. 354, Bishop Liberius of Rome ordered the people to celebrate on December 25. He probably picked that date because it was the time that citizens of Rome celebrated the Feast of Saturn, the birthday of the sun. Christmas honored Christ, instead of Saturn, as the "light of the world."

One of December's big days should be the official arrival of winter on the 21st or 22nd, depending on the position of the sun. We pay little attention to that official arrival, of course, because winter came for us when the last of autumn's bright foliage fell to the ground, when frost blackened summer's flowers and we had to light the first fire of the season or turn up the furnace. Sometimes December isn't particularly win-try-feeling. Cool weather even brings out some flowers — camellias and sasanquas and the fragrant narcissi in some parts of the South. The evergreen pyracantha, yaupon, and hollies are loaded with red berries, and those gardeners lucky enough to have the lovely tea olive somewhere in their yard may bring in a sprig or two of the pale yellow blossoms with their heart-stopping fragrance.

But there can be a day — and oh, what a day — when the temperature drops, the skies grow gray and sullen, and a bitter, biting wind blows. "Getting to be Christmasy weather," we tell one another happily. Irving Berlin never wrote a Christmas song to *that* kind of weather, but if you are a Southerner you love it, not because it is particularly pleasant, but because it is one more evidence of something we take pride in — weather like Shakespeare's Cleopatra, a creature of infinite variety.

A year or so ago I spent Thanksgiving down in Biloxi on the gulf coast where the sun shone steadily, constantly, unremittingly, like its life depended on it. The sky was a deep and flawless blue. The water in the bay looked like glass and showed only a gentle ripple or two as the tide came in and then reversed itself.

"Have you ever seen more beautiful weather?" somebody asked about once an hour, and we all dutifully looked at it and pronounced it perfect.

The truth is that I'm not really crazy about perfect weather. I mean, it's fine if you don't have too much of it. It's like those deathless, plastic flowers — monotonous, totally boring — if it happens too often or for too long a time.

Then I came home and my kind of weather set in — the marvelous, changing, awful, beautiful weather that North Georgia serves up as a regular thing. Right away I found the house so cool I needed a fire in the fireplace. The sky was suitably overcast, the trees looked suitably wintery bare, and there was a promise of rain in the air.

At 3 A.M. I awakened to hear it on the roof, pecking lightly at the old white oak shakes like a covey of persistent birds. I had two choices, both of them pleasant: I could pull up another blanket and go back to sleep, or I could go put on the coffee pot and poke my head outdoors and smell and taste the rain. As little rain as I'd been seeing, I couldn't risk not enjoying it to the fullest. And it was a good thing, because it hadn't set out to thrum away at the housetop all day. It slacked up and started again and drifted away and came back.

By the time I headed for the bus stop, the earth was soggy, the sky was dark, a chill wind blew, and we all grinned happily at one another and promised ourselves we were going to have a regular downpour any minute.

The bus came and all of us who had waited together huddled deeper in our raincoats and talked about Christmas. There's nothing like good, nasty weather to get you in the mood for Christmas shopping.

Traffic to town was heavy. Lights in store windows which had looked impotent and a little tawdry in last week's brilliant sunshine now looked jolly and festive.

My kind of weather, particularly for December.

Once I had a greenhouse, a marvelous structure of plastic film stretched over black, plastic pipes which had been bent into the shape of arches. We got the pattern from the University of Georgia School of Agriculture, and for several years that greenhouse was the joy of my life, particularly in December when I couldn't garden outside. Every movable plant was lugged inside and kept warm by a little kerosene heater. Then that heater went beserk and killed everything in its charge with a coating of evil, black soot. So we ran pipes and installed a little propane heater, which worked fine but became useless when the plastic roof was ripped off by a boisterous breeze.

Someday, someday, I mumbled, I will have a proper, glass-enclosed greenhouse. The first step in that direction was a sort of elongated-window greenhouse built over the seldom-used door which opened from the little hall connecting the two log cabins to the brick terrace in the side yard. It was a lovesome thing, that diminutive green-"house." For a couple of years. I spent halcyon hours in the fall potting plants to save over, and enticing moments in late winter starting seeds in little foil pie pans, all to grow in strength and greenness in that pint-sized glass house. (I still call it the Crystal Palace.) Then an unforeseen calamity, a record-breaking December freeze, got those plants.

So now I'm back to window gardening. A kitchen window in the country is a wondrous thing — better than rubies and diamonds. I liked my kitchen window when I lived in the city, admired the sun rising over my neighbor's rooftop. But having a window which looks out on woods and a view of the sun coming up beyond a little hill and a big oak tree is worth a great deal. A little pot of chives and a pot of paperwhite narcissus coming into bloom furnish the sill handsomely. The Christmas cactus in the old salt crock has never bloomed, but it looks healthy and promising this year. The little white vinegar and oil pitchers, which one of my daughters brought me from the Biltmore Hotel's going-out-of-business sale, hold mixed bouquets of things I hope will take root — Swedish ivy, coleus, wandering Jew, and slips of the now defunct geraniums.

Beyond the window, the country begins with the sweep of brown grass, the hill rising toward the woods, the spare brown and gray beauty of the December

[141]

landscape. One year I made a Christmas tree for the birds, and I think about it again — dipping pine cones in melted suet, studding them with seeds, and hanging them from the gnarled, old peach tree branches like ornaments. I worried that the swaying of the cones would discourage the birds, but they apparently love to bat them with their beaks, grabbing seeds and suet on the wing. The little birds — nuthatches, titmice, and juncos — light on the cones and on baskets which I made out of orange skins and filled with peanut butter. One beautiful, big, redheaded woodpecker spent ten minutes sort of lounging on a branch and eating from a cone that the wind had wound around until it was within easy reach. The mockingbirds and the cardinals, too heavy to light on the tree ornaments, pretended that they were hummingbirds and ate poised in midair. They came in great numbers in the early morning, complaining like high-paying guests that the water in the shell on the terrace was frozen and I hadn't replaced it. I have a big tea kettle, and I keep it filled for such exigencies. If the pipes should freeze, I'd still have enough water for the birds — and my coffee pot.

The approach of Christmas accentuates every mood, I suppose. A woman wrote me a long letter about the grief and pain of living and ended with the prediction that I probably would not understand it.

"You have probably never cried yourself to sleep at night," she wrote. "I'm sure strong people don't."

Of course I have the middle-of-the-nights. Of course I cry, and I have never professed to be one of those strong people she mentioned. But even very strong people are not immune to hurts.

A wise and good woman I know, now in her eighties, presents a cheerful countenance to the world out of pride and a certain religious belief. She doesn't think it becomes a believer in God to show a doleful face to the world.

"Don't you ever cry and butt your head against the wall? Don't you screech and kick your feet and curse?" I once asked her.

She smiled her gentle smile and said, "My dear, would our blessed Lord want that?"

"Oh, I guess not," I said hastily. And then she patted me on the shoulder.

"I have my sad times," she said softly. "I'm ashamed of it but sometimes I give up hope — for just a little while — and then I cry. I don't think it is heresy. Despair is that. I think we wouldn't have been given tears if we weren't intended to shed them."

It made me feel better, and I hope it made the young woman who wrote me feel better. Cry if you have to, if you need to, if it helps. And don't be ashamed of it as weakness.

We are easy criers in my family. We cry because something is pretty or it evokes a memory. We cry because we are happy. We cry over brides and babies and funerals, over music and flags and stars. We cry when we meet and sometimes when we part. We cry out of happiness and grief and loneliness. Tears well up and we get red-nosed and snuffly, but usually we feel better afterwards.

Maybe tears of self-pity are wrong. Maybe you are indulging yourself and becoming sappy and mawkish when you beat your breast and howl, "Oh, woe is me!" But that sure helps sometimes.

Celestine Sibley

There comes a time every December when, worka-day cares and tasks aside, you suddenly are aware of the specialness of this month — the Christmas feeling, I think it is. It hits you at different times, but looking back, I can almost remember those times for dozens of years. Sometimes it comes late, when you are tired and discouraged and feel hopelessly behind on all your projects and out-of-joint with the festivity which you know to be brewing all around you. Sometimes a warm rush of gladness and excitement over Christmas hits you with a wallop in an unexpected place.

Once when it hit I was on a bus trying to struggle home with two little red rockers I hadn't thought I would be able to buy. Another time it came when we unpacked the Christmas tree ornaments and took out battered and well-loved things.

One year, in the midst of many projects and prob-lems, I thought I might have to totter through the season without that sustaining wave of pre-Christmas excitement and delight. Get through it somehow, I thought resignedly, do what is necessary, be as happy as possible, and don't count on choking up with joy unconfined. My grandchildren, Bird and Tib, now grown up, were young enough then to go to a day-care center after school every day to wait for one or the other of their parents to pick them up. I was asked to get them one bleak December day, and I went in my old pickup truck to the little house in Ansley Park where they waited. I felt rushed and tired and distracted. The children came out looking rosy-cheeked and sparkly-eyed from play and clutching a cookie in each hand.

They climbed into the truck making sounds of approval for their favorite vehicle. Then they saw a Christmacy-looking box I had on the seat beside me.

"It's open," Tib reported delightedly. "Can we look?"

[144]

"I guess so," I said, my mind on the traffic and the on-coming headlights which were beginning to blind me.

I heard a soft inrush of breath from Tib, and then Bird cried, "Nestes! Nestes for the Christmas tree!"

There was one for each of us — little gold nests made of excelsior, with a clothespin attached to hold it to the Christmas tree, and a bright plumaged bird with three, tiny, glass ornament eggs on each nest. A note on each said:

> *Especially blessed*
> *And happy is he,*
> *Who finds a bird's nest*
> *In his Christmas tree.*
> *—Old Swedish proverb.*

Our long-time friend, Jo Severinghaus, had made them for us. It took a mile or so for them to pick out the bird they each wanted. They lingered over the decision and finally settled on a pink bird for Tib and a yellow one for Bird.

And then they started singing — not together, of course, but two different songs. It was "Silent Night" from Bird and "O Tannenbaum" from Tib. I shushed them and started them over, and we all sang together, "Silent night, holy night, all is calm, all is bright . . ."

Suddenly that December twilight was calm and bright. The darkness coming on had a velvety look. Traffic lights twinkled like stars. The voices of the children rose sweetly — off-key and out of time but lovely. Christmas, I thought ah, Christmas . . . it's here.

Christmas

MY MOTHER MUV was bad about not practicing what she preached. She admonished me never to speak to strangers and to be careful about the caliber of my friends, for you are judged, she contended, by the company you keep. To hear her tell it, nobody in the great outside world was safe for me to talk to except "men in brass buttoms" — policemen and firemen, of course — and, if you were desperate and had to ask for directions or help, a man who wore the insignia of the Masonic order.

As a child I heard all that and heeded it. My mother did not.

She regularly picked up strangers on street corners, or trains, and on buses. Once she fell into conversation with an old lady on the Dauphin Street trolley and brought her home. The old lady, a gentle, myopic soul who couldn't remember where she lived, stayed three weeks.

Not many months before she died, my mother became so thick with a soldier she met on an airplane that she was invited to attend his wedding. I think she would have gone but for the prohibitive price of airfare to Wichita. (She thought it was a town in France.)

Once when she was hostess to her beloved WSCS (Women's Society for Christian Service, the old name for the Methodist women's group), she invited the town's only known prostitute to join them for lunch.

"But Muv, she's . . ." I sputtered, aghast. "What did the others . . .?"

"She's my friend," my mother said firmly. "She's always treated me well. And if you were going to ask, what did the others say, what could they say? She was my guest and this is my house."

But it was not just her house or just her guest that Christmas day during the Depression when she invited a tramp to have Christmas dinner with us. We were accustomed to feeding what my father called Weary Willies, the great fraternity of jobless, often homeless men who beat their way across the country on freight trains, looking, looking — for jobs, for a bed, for a meal. Many of them came to our door, offering to cut wood or hoe the garden or do any work at all for a meal. Muv never turned one away empty-handed. Sometimes our larder offered slim pickings, but if there were anything at all in the house — a few cold biscuits, some baked sweet potatoes, apples or eggs — my mother handed it out the back door.

We knew she would do that, and because it seemed important to her, we accepted it. A friend who suggested that she was motivated by superstition, fearing that if we didn't help we, too, would fall upon hard times and hunger, got no argument from Muv.

"Sure," she said, "As ye sow . . ."

Then on Christmas morning, a particularly unattractive tramp showed up at the front gate.

The smell of a baking hen and cornbread dressing, rich with homegrown onions and sage, perfumed the frosty air. There was a big fire in the living room fireplace, and the wood heater in the dining room glowed rosily, sending out warmth from its corner. Muv had set the table with the best cloth and dishes the night before, lamenting that having only three places didn't make it a festive board. Apples from a cousin in Virginia, polished to a satiny sheen, blazed like mammoth rubies in the center of the table. I knew that on a cold shelf in the pantry that best-of-all Christmas desserts, ambrosia, waited in Grandma's cut glass bowl to be served with Muv's nut cake. (We had plenty of pecans that year, but the high cost of citron and candied cherries and pineapple made real fruitcake a casualty of the Depression.)

My Santa Claus presents had engrossed me all morning, but you can stretch your delight in a game and a book and some beads and a bracelet just so far, so I was beginning to anticipate the next major attraction on the day's program — Christmas dinner. That's when our hound dog Bertha began barking languidly (Bertha was not a very spirited watchdog) and we heard a gruff "Hello!" from the front gate. My father and I went to the door.

A scruffy little man in filthy khaki pants, recognizing Bertha's lackadaisical attitude toward watchdogging, was coming up the walk. He carried the tramp's inevitable croker sack over his shoulder.

"Howdy, neighbor," he said, drawing close enough for me to get a whiff of the stench of unwashed body and clothes, old grease, the acrid smell of train smoke, and something worse that I was too young to identify.

"Neighbor?" I thought with the scorn of the young. "We don't have any filthy neighbors like that."

He had mentioned food, and my father was directing him to the back door in automatic concern for Muv's clean floors when Muv came up behind us.

"Merry Christmas!" she called. "Come in, come in!"

We looked at her in amazement. Tramps always came to the back door and ate what she had to offer on the back steps.

The tramp himself was apparently startled to be welcomed at the front of the house. He looked at his broken shoes, one of them bound around with a dirty rag to hold the sole in place.

"Oh, ma'am," he said, "I wouldn't want to track up your floors."

"That's perfectly all right," Muv said cordially. "I can have clean floors any time. This is Christmas, and we want you to have Christmas dinner with us."

The man stared at her in surprise, and I saw for the first time that one of his eyes, half hidden by the slouch brim of his battered, black felt hat, was as white and blank as a porcelain doorknob. My father turned to look at her and then he rallied.

"Yes, yes," he said. "Come right in to the fire."

They must have exchanged names. I know that my father took the visitor to the little room we called the washroom, which antedated a real bathroom, and carried a kettle of hot water to him. Muv hurried to set another place at the table. Presently we were seated, had bowed our heads for the blessing, and were waiting expectantly for that lovely ritual of carving the fowl. I looked at the man across from me and thought he must be the ugliest person in the world, gnomelike and twisted in body, the face beneath that repulsive blank eye stretched and puckered in a hideous scar. And he still smelled.

Muv appeared not to notice, although, if it had been me, she would have sent me in search of more hot water and lye soap. She asked the usual bright and sociable questions. Where was he from? Where was he going? Did he have family?

At first he said little, applying himself to chicken and dressing and sweet potatoes and the beans and squash Muv had put up in the summer with this meal in mind. He ate rapidly but neatly, and after a time he leaned back from the table and told Muv the things she was